LITERATURE REVISION NOTES AND EXAMPLES

A MIDSUMMER NIGHT'S DREAM

by
D.C. Perkins
and I. Huke

CELTIC REVISION AIDS

CELTIC REVISION AIDS
Mayfield Road,
Walton-on-Thames, Surrey, KT12 5PL

©C.E.S. Ltd.

First published 1981

ISBN 017 751305 5

Printed in Hong Kong

Authors' Preface

This book is one of a series planned to help students working to pass public examinations. The object of each book in the series is twofold. Firstly, the book provides clarification and evaluation of each set work: biographical and historical facts and critical discussion of each work are included. Secondly, it serves as a revision aid useful for pinpointing recall just prior to an examination.

Ideally, this book should be used with and alongside the set work as it is studied. In this way it will serve to amplify and complement the work under consideration whether it be an anthology, a lyrical or narrative poem, a series of essays or short stories, a play, a novel or other form of literary expression. Those studying on their own for R.S.A., Chamber of Commerce, C.S.E., G.C.E. O Level or 16+ examinations will find it especially useful.

For those who require more advanced knowledge and who are studying for more senior examinations, such as A Level or Scottish Highers, additional material as well as worked examples, problem themes, and more searching questions are included. These are introduced to stimulate and encourage the further reading that is necessary beyond 16+.

D.C.P.
I.H.

Note on the text

The text used is the New Penguin Shakespeare.

CONTENTS

SHAKESPEARE'S LIFE

LIFE

Little is known about the life of William Shakespeare and no biography of him was written until nearly a century after he died. For three hundred years research has been undertaken to fill in the gaps left in the story of his life in Stratford and London but nevertheless the portrait of him remains substantially unaltered. The known facts about him are given below.

William Shakespeare was the son of John Shakespeare and Mary Arden of Stratford-upon-Avon. His father and mother were married in 1558, the year Elizabeth I ascended the throne. There were eight children and William was the eldest son, there being two older sisters, Joan and Margaret.

The exact date of his birth is still not known with certainty but the usual date given is 23rd April 1564. What we do know from parish records is that William was christened in Stratford Church on the 26th April 1564. He was to live for 52 years and peculiarly enough he died on an anniversary of his supposed birth (23rd April 1616).

William's father, John, has been variously described as a glover, farmer and butcher but it is more probable that he was a dealer in wool and leather. He was a prosperous burgess (freeman of the borough) and tradesman of Stratford and lived in a house in Henley Street revered today as the birthplace of his famous son. John Shakespeare's wife, Mary Arden, was the daughter of a family of small landowners in the neighbourhood of Stratford. After his marriage, John Shakespeare became prominent in Stratford: in 1565 he was chosen as an alderman and in 1568 he held the chief municipal office of bailiff. As bailiff he was also a Justice of the Peace and in corporation documents he is mentioned as 'Master Shakespeare'.

No facts are known about the childhood and boyhood of William Shakespeare. He was probably educated at the grammar school in Stratford where education was provided free for the sons of burgesses. We know for certain that William married an Anne (or Agnes) Hathaway – a licence was issued for this event on 27th November 1582. His wife was the daughter of a yeoman-farmer and came from the hamlet of Shottery in the parish of Old Stratford. According to the evidence on her tombstone Anne Hathaway was eight years older than her husband. The actual date and place of the marriage are not known.

From the parish register we learn that a daughter, Susanna, was born to the couple; she was christened on 26th May 1583. Twins were born later and christened Hamnet and Judith, these names being entered on the parish register on 2nd February, 1583.

The years 1585-92 are a blank as far as our knowledge of Shakespeare's activities are concerned. We do know, however, that his father's fortunes declined. He had become irregular in his contributions to the town levies, he had to raise money on mortgage and he no longer attended corporation meetings. In 1586 he was removed from the list of aldermen.

It is assumed that William Shakespeare went to London in the 1580s. In September 1592 a literary attack was made upon him in *Greene's Groatsworth of Wit.* In this sixteenth-century pamphlet Greene speaks of 'an upstart crow, beautified with our feathers, that with his Tygers hart wrapt in a Players hyde, supposes he is well able to bombast out a blanke verse as the best of you, and being an absolute Johannes fac totum [i.e. Jack of all trades] is in his owne conceit the onely shack-scene in the country.' This invective was followed soon after by an apology to him by a man named Chettle who confirmed that he was well known for his 'upright dealing' and 'grace in writing'. During this period of Shakespeare's life it is clear that he wrote and remodelled plays which were produced by several companies of players including Burbage's and Alleyn's. In 1593 and 1594 Shakespeare published two poems himself. The first of these was *Venus and Adonis* and the second *The Rape of Lucrece.*

In 1594 the Lord Chamberlain's Company came into being and Shakespeare became a member of it and remained so certainly until his retirement. In 1603, when it was reconstituted, nine actors were named as shareholders in the letters patent. Shakespeare was the second on the list and the Globe Theatre was mentioned as the main place for performances. The actors belonging to the Company were ranked as Grooms of the Chamber and could be called upon to do duty as ushers at Court. For this they were paid regular stipends and received red liveries for Court performances.

Two specific events are known to have taken place in 1596. First, Shakespeare's son Hamnet died at the age of eleven. Second, a grant of family arms was applied for at the Heralds' Office. This was in the name of John Shakespeare but it is more than probable that Shakespeare applied in his father's name. In May 1597 William Shakespeare bought New Place, the largest house in Stratford-upon-Avon, for £60. After his father's death in 1601 he bought other property in the town but it is clear that during this time he stayed in London while his wife and daughters remained in Stratford. From records we can trace Shakespeare living near the Bear Garden in Southwark (1596); he was rated for a house in St. Helen's, Bishopsgate, (1597) and from

1599-1608 he lived on Bankside in Southwark. In 1604 he also spent some time as a lodger in Cripplegate. In September 1608 Shakespeare's mother died and he inherited the Henley Street properties in Stratford.

During the last eight years of his life, Shakespeare returned to Stratford and took part in local affairs. His retirement did not mean an absolute break with London. In 1613 he devised an impressa (or emblem) to be painted by Richard Burbage, and worn by the Earl of Rutland annually at the tournament on Accession Day. In the same year he bought a freehold house in Blackfriars and mortgaged it for £60. Both the freehold and the mortgage bear his signature. In March 1613 he was probably in London when his Company gave approximately 20 performances for the wedding of Princess Elizabeth and the Elector Palatinate; eight of the plays performed were Shakespeare's. His elder daughter, Susanna, had married a Stratford physician, John Hall, on 5th June 1607 and his younger daughter, Judith, married Thomas Quiney on 10th February 1616. At this time Shakespeare made his last will and testament and by April of the same year he was dead. As a tithe owner Shakespeare was buried in the chancel of the parish church. The doggerel verse on the gravestone in the chancel, and which local tradition assigns to him, reads:

> Good friend for Jesus sake forbeare,
> To digg the dust encloased heare!
> Blest be ye man yt spares thes stones,
> And curst be he yt moves my bones.

A number of conjectures of doubtful validity about Shakespeare have been made from time to time. The most important of these are:

(1) W. Beeston, an actor, whose father had been in the Lord Chamberlain's Company in 1603, recounted that Shakespeare had been a schoolmaster in the Company and went to London at 18. He acted 'exceedingly well', was a 'handsome well shaped man' and very good in company. According to this source, Shakespeare had a relationship with the wife of John D'Avenant, the Oxford vintner.

(2) A local tradition that he was involved in deer-poaching in the grounds of Sir Thomas Lucy was first suggested in the notes of Richard Davies, rector of Saperton.

(3) A third rumour was that he was an apprentice butcher in Stratford and ran away to London where he became a servitor (apprentice) in a playhouse.

(4) Another account says that his first job in London was to hold horses for gentlemen who came to the playhouse and then he became a prompter.

(5) According to another tradition Shakespeare was a much better poet than actor.

These traditions need to be treated cautiously, although it does seem certain that Shakespeare never played principal parts.

WORKS

The following chronology is based on Sir Edmund Chambers' *William Shakespeare: a Study of Facts and Problems* (1930) and it is only approximate. Later research has tended to push back the dates of the earlier plays.

1590-91	1.	*Henry VI, Part II*
	2.	*Henry VI, Part III*
1591-92	3.	*Henry VI, Part I*
	4.	*Richard III*
	5.	*The Comedy of Errors*
1593-94	6.	*Titus Andronicus*
	7.	*The Taming of the Shrew*
1594-95	8.	*The Two Gentlemen of Verona*
	9.	*Love's Labour Lost*
	10.	*Romeo and Juliet*
1595-96	11.	*Richard II*
	12.	*A Midsummer Night's Dream*
1596-97	13.	*King John*
	14.	*The Merchant of Venice*
1597-98	15.	*Henry IV, Part I*
	16.	*Henry IV, Part II*
	17.	*Much Ado about Nothing*
	18.	*Henry V*
1599-1600	19.	*Julius Caesar*
	20.	*As You Like It*
	21.	*Twelfth Night*
1600-01	22.	*Hamlet*
	23.	*The Merry Wives of Windsor*
1601-02	24.	*Troilus and Cressida*
1602-03	25.	*All's Well That Ends Well*
1604-05	26.	*Measure for Measure*
	27.	*Othello*
1605-06	28.	*King Lear*
	29.	*Macbeth*
1606-07	30.	*Antony and Cleopatra*
1607-08	31.	*Coriolanus*
	32.	*Timon of Athens*

1608-09	33.	*Pericles*
1609-10	34.	*Cymbeline*
1610-11	35.	*The Winter's Tale*
1611-12	36.	*The Tempest*
1612-13	37.	*Henry VIII*
	38.	*The Two Noble Kinsmen*

As far as non-dramatic work is concerned Shakespeare's work consists of two narrative poems, contributions to two anthologies, the sonnets and, of course, the songs which appear in many of the plays. The narrative poems dedicated to the Earl of Southampton were *Venus and Adonis* (entered on the Stationer's Register on 18th April 1593) and *The Rape of Lucrece* (9th May 1594). It is probable that these were written between June 1592 and April 1594 because the theatres in London were closed, first because of riots and then because of plague. The stories in these narrative poems come from Ovid's *Metamorphoses* and *Fusti* respectively and they contain signs of the poetic genius that was to show more clearly in the later plays. The minor poems occur in *The Passionate Pilgrim,* a poetic miscellany published by William Jaggard, and *Diverse Poetical Essaies,* published by Sir Robert Chester in 1601.

The most outstanding non-dramatic work is the 150 sonnets published by the stationer Thomas Thorpe on 20th May 1609. Shakespearean scholars have given these sonnets a great deal of attention and controversy has arisen over their character, their date and literary history. The first 126 are addressed to a young man, the poet's friend and patron, who may be Mr. W.H., the 'lovely boy' referred to in the poetry. The remaining sonnets seem to record the poet's relations with a mistress, a dark-haired woman with mournful eyes. Scholars on the whole consider that the sonnets are autobiographical but even after years of argument this has not been conclusively established. Finally, there are the songs. Occurring in many plays, especially the comedies, they show a variety of moods and a freshness of tone and are some of the best-loved of Shakespeare's lyrical poetry.

Shakespeare's dramatic work can be conveniently considered in five stages:

1590-96

These were years of dramatic apprenticeship in which Shakespeare wrote plays similar in style to those of his rivals. An affected literary style, known as 'euphuism', derived from John Lyly's prose romance *Euphues.* Euphuists attached great importance to the balance of words, phrases and sentences, other characteristics being prolonged alliteration, allusions to classical mythology from Greek and Roman times, lengthy similes and elaborate metaphors. Sentences were complicated but very skilfully controlled. The artificiality of speech and decorative effects are evident in such lines as:

> Read o'er the volume of young Paris' face
> And find delight, writ there with beauty's pen.
> Examine every married lineament,
> And see how one another lends content:
> And what obscured in this fair volume lies,
> Find written in the margent of his eyes.

(Romeo and Juliet)

1596-1601

By this time, Shakespeare had discarded the artificial form of writing found in the earlier plays; indeed he begins to make fun of the euphuistic writers. He is now writing fluently and confidently. His genius is at its height in the romantic comedies – *As You Like It, Twelfth Night* and *Much Ado About Nothing.* Rhyme is used only when there is a quite definite dramatic reason for using it. Besides the comedies the English historical plays belong to this period.

1601-09

In this later period Shakespeare shows all the versatility that he had learned in his earlier years. He had mastered his medium and moves easily from scenes of comedy and mirth to scenes of pathos and tragedy. The distinctive feature in this group of plays is their concentration of thought. The images are piled up one on another in order to convey shades of emotion and an intensity of feeling that had never been attempted before:

> Here lay Duncan,
> His silver skin laced with his golden blood;
> And his gash'd stabs look'd like a breach in nature
> For ruin's wasteful entrance: there, the murderers,
> Steep'd in the colours of their trade, their daggers
> Unmannerly breech'd with gore.

(Macbeth, Act II, Scene 3)

1609-13

These last plays are of a complex romantic and magical type and were written principally for the new indoor theatre at Blackfriars. The staging is more complicated, using the technical resources of the new theatre. Because of his established reputation, Shakespeare's plays were now being performed before distinguished audiences and this is to some extent reflected in elaborate staging and special effects.

From time to time 'new' plays written by Shakespeare have been 'discovered'. A case in point is *The Booke of Sir Thomas More* which has been attributed to various of Shakespeare's contemporaries. The latest attempt to attribute authorship to Shakespeare was undertaken by computer analysis in 1980. The method involved examination of various stylistic elements in the play, called 'word habits' and compared these with 'word habits' in other of Shakespeare's plays. Although 41 were found to be the same as in *Julius Caesar, Pericles* and *Titus Andronicus,* the claim has received little scholastic approval as the system of comparing in this way and the plays chosen for comparison are not considered objective.

The analysis above can only be a generalisation and oversimplification and it is hoped that the interested student will read further on Shakespeare's dramatic art and its development. Dr Johnson put it succinctly: 'Shakespeare's plays are not in the rigorous and critical sense either tragedies or comedies, but compositions of a distinct kind; exhibiting the real state of sublunary nature, which partakes of good and evil, joy and sorrow, mingled with endless variety of proportion and innumerable modes of combination.'

(Preface to Shakespeare's Works)

THE ELIZABETHAN THEATRE

Every artist has to work in his chosen medium, and Shakespeare is a supreme example of such an artist. He wrote for the stage in the late 16th and early 17th centuries and thus it is vital to know as much as we can about the theatres, the actors and audience of his generation – it is important to appreciate the advantages they had as well as the limitations.

By the 16th century a tradition of acting was very well established. In the Middle Ages morality and miracle plays depicting biblical themes were the vogue and the folk play inspired actors and audiences alike. The nobility began to maintain small groups of entertainers and these actors were often skilled swordsmen, wrestlers, dancers, musicians and singers. The Elizabethan stage inherited the religious traditions, the expertise of the actors and the custom of service to a patron.

James Burbage built the first theatre, called the 'Theatre', in 1576 but until that time Elizabethan actors performed on a variety of stages. Thus they:
(1) performed in noblemen's houses or mansions – the great halls and long galleries were useful for this purpose;
(2) performed in the Queen's residences or palaces;
(3) gave plays in the Inns of Court;
(4) acted in Town Halls;
(5) acted in inn yards.

Actors had begun to travel in groups, or troupes, and made themselves available for hire. The nobility encouraged them to travel around and although the actors still owed them a certain allegiance they had a measure of independence from their benefactors. Realising that there was a steady market for the performances, especially in the large towns and London, the actors hired inn yards and other suitable spaces for their plays. In London they gave performances on the roads leading into and out of the city. Typical inns were the Saracen's Head in Islington, the Boar's Head and the Red Lion in Whitechapel and the Tabard in Southwark. These stood on the routes from the north, east and south into the city and London theatre inns became established; for example, we know of the Bell, the Bull, the Cross Keys and the Bel Savage.

These itinerant actors thus moved from place to place carrying a waggon-load of costumes, properties and play-books, seeking a place to perform. Once this had been agreed, they set up a simple stage. This was merely a platform of boards resting on trestles or barrels with a curtained booth at the back. In this curtained section the actors would change their costumes and await their cues. From the occupation of an inn yard it was only a short step to the occupation of an entire inn and then to the building of a purpose-built theatre.

Modern reconstructions of the Elizabethan stage depend upon guesswork based on the following evidence:

(1) The Swan drawing – a contemporary sketch of the Elizabethan stage made by a Dutchman named Johannes de Witt. He made a sketch of the Swan Theatre which was copied by his friend Arend Von Buchel.

(2) Stage directions.

(3) The contract to build the theatre called the 'Fortune'.

The new theatres were obliged by law to be built in the suburbs. Thus, the Theatre and the Curtain (both built in 1576) were in Moorfields near Shoreditch; the Rose (1587), the Swan (1595), The Globe (1598) and the Hope (1613) were built in the heart of Southwark on the south bank of the Thames; the Fortune (1599) was near Cripplegate, and the Red Bull (1605) was in Clerkenwell. Most of these theatres were owned by investors who rented them to companies of actors. Shakespeare's company was unusual in that the actors owned the theatre. The Globe was erected at the joint expense of the troupe, including James Burbage and Shakespeare himself, and this was followed by the same actors leasing a theatre in Blackfriars in 1608. The Blackfriars, as it was called, was a hall with adjacent rooms converted to theatrical use and was admirable as an indoor theatre; the Globe, open to the sky, was suitable for summer entertainment.

From the evidence that exists we know that Elizabethan theatres were small. Externally circular or octagonal, they measured about 80 square feet outside and internally about 55 feet. The stage occupied almost half the area inside. Despite the fact that there were differences between the theatres (for example the Globe and the Blackfriars) we can describe a typical open-air theatre, bearing in mind that controversy and conjecture still abound.

The stage was raised and jutted out into the yard or pit; this was called an 'apron stage'. The audience stood in the pit, which was open to the sky, and into which the stage projected, and wealthier spectators were accommodated in roofed galleries built in the theatre walls. A few bought stools on the stage itself or sat on it. The stage was strewn with rushes to keep the actors from slipping. One gallery overhung the stage at the back. At the back also were the tiring rooms of the actors. There the actors could keep their properties, costumes and play-books. It was from the back that actors made their entrances and exits.

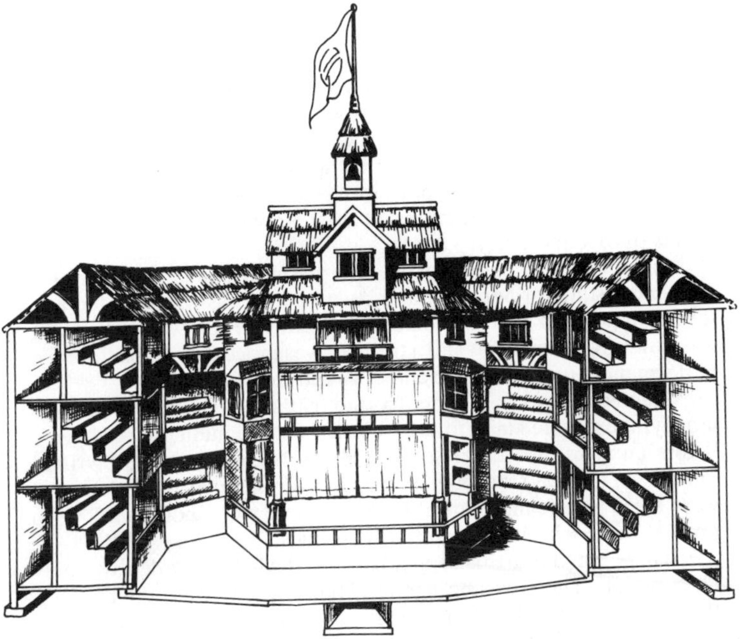

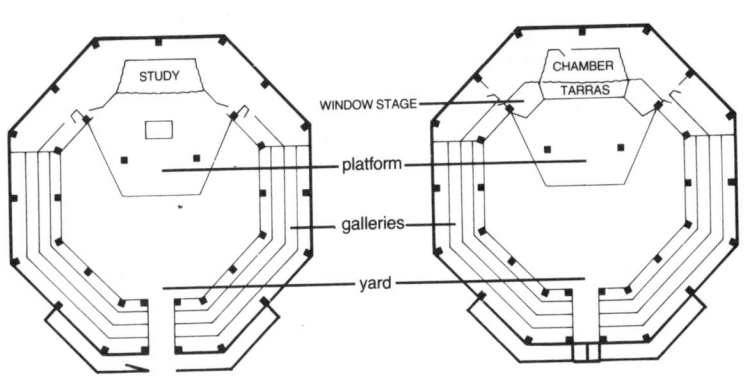

The Playhouse – Ground plan   The Playhouse – Tarras level

The stage itself was hung with arras (tapestry) and there were no side or drop curtains.

In the stage wall there were three openings at the back. The centre opening was larger than the other two and could be curtained off when desired. Above was a balcony which served for castle walls, an upper room and such-like accommodation. Over the whole stage a canopy, or 'shadow', acted as an umbrella for the actors; it was fastened to posts resting on the stage. Trapdoors were concealed in the stage-floor, connecting with the tiring rooms at the rear and affording additional means of exit and entry.

Plays were performed in the afternoon, usually beginning at 2 p.m. and lasting for approximately two hours. Bills were printed and set up on posts as advertisements. When the theatre was open a flag was flown from the turret and a trumpet was thrice sounded before the performance; on the third trumpet sound the play began.

Admission was paid on entry and 'gatherers' used to collect the money; there were stairs to the galleries and the audience paid again before entry to the dearer seats. The actors could consult a written synopsis of the play (the 'platt') which hung from a peg, 'stage-keepers' were there to give mechanical help and there were 'book-holders' to prompt those who had forgotten their lines.

There was no artificial lighting and daylight afforded the only illumination. There was no need for the actors to raise their voices, they were in the midst of their audience and soliloquies presented no problems because the audience could hear every word.

There was no scenery except an occasional property – a gate; a notice or a tree – and there were no realistic sound effects. The action was continuous. A scene ended when all the actors had left the stage and a new set of characters entered. Continuity was therefore maintained and it was hard to break the illusion. Whenever it was necessary to identify the exact location of a particular scene the appropriate description and details were given aloud by one of the characters. Simple properties or garments were used to illustrate particular scenes. Thus a chair or stool showed an indoor scene; a soldier wearing armour represented a battlefield; a watchman carrying a lantern or a person wearing a nightcap indicated a night-scene or a man wearing riding boots was a messenger. Properties were used to replace scenery and they were many and varied – beds, benches, tables, thrones, gibbets, cauldrons, hatchets, feathers, wooden targets, lions' heads, crowns, helmets and shields, to name only a few. Costumes were often lavish and imposing and an inventory of costumes in the *Henslowe Papers* lists 84 garments of various kinds such as 'a cardinal's gown' and 'a crimson robe striped with gold and faced with ermine'. Despite this, plays were not acted in period costume and there was little attempt at historical accuracy – the Romans in *Julius Cæsar* wore doublets, cloaks and large Elizabethan-style hats. Throughout the plays alarums, retreats, flourishes and other signals were sounded on trumpets.

The actors themselves were competent people. Play-acting was a regular feature of Tudor education and by the time they were on the London stage the actors were obviously proficient. Plays were normally acted on the repertory system and the average life of a new play was about ten performances. The Elizabethan actors in a particular theatre comprised a permanent 'fellowship of players' and they worked on the share system. A playwright had to write parts to suit the members of his fellowship, and to fit their physical and acting characteristics. Thus in many of the plays physical types recur. A tall man with a thin face appears as Shadow in *Henry IV, Part II,* as Sir Andrew Aguecheek in *Twelfth Night,* as Slender in *The Merry Wives of Windsor* and as Monsieur le Beau in *As You Like It.* Will Kempe who took the part of the clown in Shakespeare's Company was well known as a comedian who specialised in bawdy humour and danced jigs. Shakespeare undoubtedly had him in mind for Peter in *Romeo and Juliet* and Dogberry in *Much Ado About Nothing.* Kempe was replaced by Robert Armin who was witty, sympathetic and quite sophisticated and thus he could take the parts of Feste, Lear's Fool and Touchstone in *As You Like It.* The 'fat' parts in the play, such as Falstaff, were written for actors like Thomas Pollard.

It is often thought that actors were nothing more than ne'er-do-wells and vagabonds and we owe much of this to the enmity of the Puritans, who were a growing religious sect. The fact is that the actor was generally respected in his own day. It is true, of course, that some of the poorer companies used untrained, illiterate and often incompetent 'hirelings' as actors but these were a far cry from the best of the day. The theatre, indeed prided itself on providing a full training for apprentices who served a leading actor or 'sharer' and in due time took singing and women's parts eventually becoming fully fledged members of the cast. It is true that women were not allowed on the stage. The parts of young women were acted by boy apprentices until their voices broke. This accounts for the few women's parts that appear in Elizabethan plays and also accounts for the number of the plays in which women disguise themselves as young men. From 1605-08 Shakespeare's Company evidently included a young boy who was well-known for playing emotional and wicked women. Shakespeare undoubtedly had him in mind when he devised Cleopatra, Goneril in *King Lear* and Lady Macbeth.

SHAKESPEAREAN STUDIES

(a) LITERARY CRITICISM

Since Shakespeare's death thousands of books have been written on his plays and poetry. Ben Jonson and John Dryden were two of the earliest critics and while they praised his achievements they disapproved of his aims and methods. In the 1700s critics were concerned with Shakespeare's education or lack of it (Richard Farmer, *Essay on the Learning of Shakespeare* and T.W. Baldwin, *William Shakespeare, Small Latine* and *Lesse Greek*.) They also wrote about what they regarded as Shakespeare's shortcomings – his failure to observe the classical unities, his puns, his anachronisms and his bawdy. Walter Whiter (in *Specimen of a Commentary on Shakespeare* 1794) was one of the first to recognise the importance of Shakespeare's creative processes and Maurice Morgann's *Essay on the Dramatic Character of Sir John Falstaff* was important because it paved the way to a consideration of the supreme importance of Shakespeare's characterisation.

William Hazlitt's *Characters of Shakespeare* (1816) continued to highlight the importance of the playwright's characters and this insistence on character prevailed throughout the 19th and 20th centuries. Coleridge and Keats entered the field and as poets themselves provided special insight into Shakespeare's creative processes. In the 19th century, too, there was some controversy over the philosophical importance of characterisation. While Victor Hugo and Swinburne were enthusiastic about Shakespeare the Victorian age was devoid of major critique but interest in Shakespeare as a poet and dramatist emerged in Walter Pater's *Appreciations*, Edmond Malone's work and Professor Edward Dowden's *Shakespeare: Critical Study of His Mind and Art* (1875).

In 1904 came A.C. Bradley's *Shakespearean Tragedy* which was the zenith of character analysis. He pursued the characters beyond the confines of the plays and showed some preoccupation with the moral reasons for tragedy. Later critics have reacted against his work. Sir Edmund Chambers in *William Shakespeare: a Study of Facts and Problems* brought to the plays a knowledge of the medieval and Elizabethan stage which was second to none; he was one of the first to study dramatic conventions. Granville-Barker's multi-volumed *Prefaces to Shakespeare* (1927-48) pinpointed Shakespeare as a play-presenter and this was followed by investigations of Elizabethan psychology.

Then it was the turn of the psychoanalysts led by J.I.M. Stewart's

Character and Motive in Shakespeare (1949) and Ernest Jones in *Hamlet and Oedipus* who was inspired by the ideas of Sigmund Freud. A return to normality was stressed in Lascelles Abercrombie's essay *A Plea for the Liberty of Interpreting Shakespeare* when he advocated freedom of interpreting the bard. This was followed by writers like John Middleton Murray, George Wilson Knight and Caroline Spurgeon who investigated the poetry and symbolism of the plays. Caroline Spurgeon, in her survey of Shakespeare's images, *Shakespeare's Imagery and what it tells us* (1935), pointed to clusters of images peculiar to Shakespeare and W.H. Clemen followed this with his book *The Development of Shakespeare's Imagery* (1951) which studied his dramatic use of metaphor.

G. Wilson Knight's thesis in his book *The Wheel of Fire* (1949) regards each play as a visionary unit and he revealed the symbolic overtones which persist in each. Nowadays criticism is characterised by close linguistic analysis which has been attacked by Rosemond Tuve in *Elizabethan and Metaphysical Imagery* (1947). A wider knowledge of the thoughts and beliefs of Shakespeare's day, as shown by E.M.W. Tillyard's book *The Elizabethan World Picture* (1943), has tended to put Shakespeare in perspective and new editions of the plays are steadily appearing.

(b) EDITING SHAKESPEARE

When Shakespeare died in 1616 only 14 of his plays were regularly in print. The rest were produced in one volume in 1623. This printed volume was known as the 'First Folio'; it included all the plays already printed except *Pericles,* 36 plays altogether.

In all of Shakespeare's texts there are difficulties caused by printing errors, meaningless sentences, meaningless phrases, reprinting and differences in spelling. To make a Shakespearean text readable, therefore, it has been necessary for scholars to edit the texts. This means that they have made alterations to and added to the originals intending to make them more intelligible to the reader. The Shakespearean play that you read is therefore an edited version of the play. Most modern texts (including the one used here) combine the clearest and fullest versions of the play from the five quartos (early printed editions of individual plays) and the Folio of 1623.

(c) ANTI-SHAKESPEAREAN THEORIES

Sir Francis Bacon

The idea that Shakespeare did not write the plays which bear his name has existed for generations. The reasons for it lie in the obvious genius of Shakespeare, as a writer, compared with his humble origin and education. About 1785 an idea originated by Rev. James Wilmot, rector of Burton on the Heath, Warwickshire, was that the plays were the work of Sir Francis Bacon, Viscount St. Albans. The first published statement of the theory was W. J. Smith's *Was Lord Bacon the Author of Shakespeare's Plays?* (1856) which began the Bacon-Shakespeare controversy. Fuel was added to the flames by I. Donnelly who in *The Great Cryptogram: Francis Bacon's Cipher in the so-called Shakespeare Plays* (1887) found ciphered messages embedded throughout the plays 'proving' Bacon's authorship. Other cryptologists followed this further until W.F. and E.S. Friedman, professionals in this field, rejected these claims as groundless – *Shakespearean Ciphers Examined* (1957).

Edward de Vere, 17th Earl of Oxford
This theory was propounded by J.T. Looney in a book entitled *Shakespeare Identified in Edward de Vere* (1920). It is said that de Vere used the assumed name of Shakespeare to protect his family from the social stigma attached to the stage.

William Stanley, 6th Earl of Derby
A.W. Titherley proposed that this man was William Shakespeare. It was suggested that Stanley concealed his identity for the same reasons as de Vere above and he retained the same initials – W.S.

Christopher Marlowe
C. Hoffman suggested that Shakespeare was really Marlowe in *The Man who was 'Shakespeare'* (1955). Because of Marlowe's avowed atheism and homosexuality he was said to have been kept safe by Sir Francis Walsingham who had someone put to death in his place and then allowed Marlowe to live and write in exile under an assumed name.

HOW TO READ AND STUDY SHAKESPEARE

A play is meant to be acted and not to be read. If possible, you should see a production of the play. If you are unable to see it on the stage, then try to see the film version. Often a production is broadcast on radio or television or there may be a tape or record of it you can listen to. If you are unable to do any of these things, ask some friends to read it with you and if possible act as you read.

Some of the allusions in the play may be lost on you but otherwise there will be much that you can understand. Thus the main story, the other stories (the 'sub-plots' as they are called), the actions and the characters will soon become familiar. The plays, although set in a different world to the one we know, consist of ideas about life in general which are as fully applicable today.

Read the play through for the first time. Then read the play again, summarising as you go along. Keep your summary short. Scenes in a play may have a purpose or a number of purposes. For example, a scene may develop the story; may develop a character; may create an atmosphere; may pass the time between two events; may give dramatic relief; may unravel the plot; or may do a variety of these. Some plays have a main character who is more important than anyone else. Shakespeare's plays often have this element, and in the tragedies, at least, these characters have a flaw in their personalities. Thus Macbeth's flaw is ambition, Hamlet's is indecision and Othello's is jealousy.

Quotations are very important, as they are often the subject of what in an examination is called a 'context question'. (Details of how to tackle this kind of question are given later.) Because of this it is important for you to incorporate in your notes as many quotations as possible.

In your summary of the play include:
(1) The essentials of the story.
(2) The part played by the main characters.
(3) The details of the personalities in the play.
(4) Their attitudes to other characters in the play.
(5) Where the climax occurs (the most important part in the play).
(6) How the plot and sub-plots are handled and how the play reaches its dénouement, or final clarification.
(7) The time span of the play.

You should now read the play again in considerably more detail. Add to your notes points on the following topics, but leave space in case anything more occurs to you later.

(1) Write one page about the story. Consider whether the story is original or whether it was copied from another writer. Shakespeare's stories, for example, are not completely original.

(2) Consider the characterisation. Is there anything which motivates the main character's action? Consider the heroes and the villains. Pick out any obvious contrasts or similarities between them.

(3) Consider the date of the play. What is its background? Consider the edition of the play and the details surrounding its appearance. Are there any difficulties of language? If there are, these will require careful attention later. Some words used by Shakespeare, for example, had different meanings for him from those they have for us. Special note must be made of these.

(4) What is the aim of the playwright? Do you think he has achieved his objective?

(5) Is it a comedy, tragedy or history? Does it try to teach us something? If there are elements of tragedy, comedy and didacticism (instruction) find which is the most important and consider how they are blended.

(6) Consider the dramatic abilities of the playwright. How does he set his scene? How does he create pathos or suspense? Does he keep the same quality throughout his play or does his writing ability vary considerably? Consider scenery, costume and movement.

(7) Is the play written in verse or prose? If written in both media, consider why this is done. How is the transformation from one to the other accomplished?

(8) One of the most important attributes of a good playwright is to handle dialogue properly. Consider how Shakespeare uses (a) dialogue, and (b) soliloquies (if there are any).

(9) Did the playwright write for a special audience or a special theatre? Shakespeare, for instance, wrote for an open-air theatre. It was special also in that no scenery was used. Some playwrights write for a satirical purpose, and there are various other types of plays, e.g. the comedy of manners, the miracle play and the morality play. Consider the use of special dramatic techniques, e.g. irony.

(10) Many playwrights have theories on dramatic art and form. Some have theories on the characters they are depicting. Find out how they evolve these theories in dramatic form.

(11) How does the play end? Do you like the ending? Do the characters deserve the reward or fate accorded them?

(12) You may be asked to give your own views on a scene or act. What impression has each part, and the whole of the play made on you?

Note: Remember that Shakespeare's plays have a definite structure. This is (a) the introduction (the setting of the scene), (b) the development of the action, (c) the climax of the play (the most important part where the play's excitement is at its most intense), and (d) the dénouement.

Remember, too, that in many of Shakespeare's comedies mistakes in identity occur. Be aware of this and be able to give reasons why they occur.

You must get to know your play really well. Ask your friends to read small quotations from the play to test your knowledge of it. Keep on reading your notes and also try to read criticisms of the play by highly regarded literary critics. Above all, find time to read the play again and again – there is no substitute for this.

Quotations are most important. If the play is in blank verse, you must quote accurately. It is a good idea to learn whole passages by heart.

(a) HOW TO ANSWER CONTEXT QUESTIONS

Context questions are detailed questions asked to ascertain whether the student knows and understands a particular novel, play or poem. Here is an example of a context question set on *Macbeth*:

> 'Tis call'd the evil;
> A most miraculous work in this good king;
> Which often, since my here-remain in England,
> I have seen him do. How he solicits heaven,
> Himself best knows: but strangely visited people.
>
> (Act IV, Scene 3)

(a) Name the speaker. What question is he answering?
(b) Who was the King of England in Macbeth's day? Is this the person referred to here?
(c) Explain the phrase 'strangely visited'.
(d) Suggest another name for the 'evil'.

This could be answered as follows:

(a) Malcolm is the speaker. He is answering Macduff's question about the nature of a disease cured by the King.
(b) The King was Edward the Confessor. It is probable that the person referred to here is King James I (1603-25) and most critics agree that this passage is one designed to praise and appeal to James.
(c) 'Strangely visited' refers to those people afflicted with uncommon diseases.
(d) The 'evil' is scrofula, which is tuberculosis of the lymphatic glands.

Context questions ask details about:
(1) the speaker of the words;
(2) to whom the words are spoken;
(3) what particular words, phrases and sentences mean;
(4) the figures of speech in the lines quoted;
(5) the importance of the quotation in the story;
(6) what the passage indicates about the characters of the speaker and the listener;
(7) how the words quoted are related to previous passages or later actions.

In some papers students are asked to paraphrase the lines or part of the passage.

Hints for the student when answering context questions.
(1) Answer the question directly.
(2) Answer in a complete sentence unless told to do otherwise.
(3) Do not refer to the extract itself as a 'context' – it is taken out of context. Call it 'the passage' or 'these lines' or 'the words'.
(4) Keep your answers as short as possible. There is no need to write at length. Quotations are not necessary in this type of answer although they are acceptable provided that they are not taken directly from the given passage.

(b) HOW TO USE QUOTATIONS

It is surprising how many students do not know how to quote properly. Many otherwise very good literature papers are spoiled because students have not been taught – or have never learned – this technique. There is a difference between quoting poetry (including blank verse) and quoting prose. When quoting poetry (or blank verse) you should take a new line. An example of this is as follows:

After this first murder Macbeth is still guided by the twin forces of ambition and fear. He believes that Banquo's offspring will be future kings and he cannot bear the thought. He says [and now comes the quotation],

> They hail'd him father to a line of kings:
> Upon my head they placed a fruitless crown,
> And put a barren sceptre in my gripe.

(Act III, Scene 1)

Note that the first letter of each word in the above is a capital. This must be retained in verse, and you must remember the exact word that starts the line. If you cannot remember a complete quotation it is quite in order to do this:

> They hail'd him father to a line of kings:
> .... a fruitless crown,
> And put a barren sceptre in my gripe.

After the quotation a new line has to be taken before continuing with your answer.

When quoting prose, however, it is **not** necessary to take a new line. You may carry on in the same line, enclosing your quotation in inverted commas. An example of this is as follows:

> Lambe said [and now the quotation in the same line], 'To be sick is to enjoy monarchal prerogatives'. He continues by saying more about people who are getting well, and affirms that getting well is 'a fall from dignity, amounting to a deposition'.

Sometimes you may find it convenient to quote short sentences or phrases in the body of the essay you are writing. This device is most useful to show that you know the play well. Here are some examples of the device in an essay on an aspect of *The Merchant of Venice:*

> Shylock is eager to have his [and now comes a small quotation] 'pound of flesh' and is pleased with Portia's assertion that a 'decree established' cannot be altered. He eagerly notes that a 'Daniel' has 'come to judgment'.

You should remember, in addition, that 'close reference' is a useful device when you cannot remember a quotation exactly or if you want to give some variety to your answers. Thus if you could not remember Hamlet's speech:

> The dread of something after death,
> The undiscovered country from whose bourn,
> No traveller returns, puzzles the will,
> And makes us rather bear the ills we have,
> Than fly to others that we know not of.
>
> (Act III, Scene 1)

it would be quite in order if you wrote:

> Hamlet speaks of the vague terrors after death, and of that unknown land from which no traveller ever comes back. He argues that this dread impedes our decisions and thus we prefer to endure our present troubles than contemplate others unknown to us.

The examiner would have no difficulty in deciding to which speech you are referring.

SOURCES OF
A MIDSUMMER NIGHT'S DREAM,
ADDITIONAL NOTES AND
MEMORY WORK

SOURCES

Most of Shakespeare's themes in his plays come from one major source in each case. For *A Midsummer Night's Dream,* however, he does not seem to have a principal source. Evidence for some sources comes from similarities between the text and any one source and similarities of incident in those sources.

1. Some of the characters and minor incidents may come from Chaucer's *The Knight's Tale* and the life of Theseus could be taken from Sir Thomas North's translation of Plutarch's *Lives of the Noble Grecians and Romans.*

2. The Pyramus and Thisbe legend is included in Ovid's *Metamorphoses* which was translated by Arthur Golding and published in 1567. Shakespeare probably owes much of his familiarity with classical mythology to this source. The 'cranny' in the wall, Ninus' tomb, the bloody mantle and the mulberry tree are alluded to in the *Metamorphoses.*

3. There is a great deal of internal evidence to suggest that several themes including the Pyramus and Thisbe story came from a poem by Thomas Mouffet called *Of the Silkwormes, and their Flies.* This poem, written between 1590 and 1595 was probably read by Shakespeare in manuscript. Shakespeare's story is so near Mouffet's version that it is usually thought to be an intentional parody of it. Shakespeare obtained the name 'Bottom' from Mouffet and copied his use of words like 'eke' and 'whereat'.

4. The Romance called *Huon of Bordeaux* is another probable source. From this source Oberon could have been derived for here the fairy is described as the three-foot-high king of the fairies in Momur.

5. Some hints for *A Midsummer Night's Dream* may also have come from John Lyly's *Endimion* and Green's portrait of Oberon in *James IV.* Also, in a Spanish prose romance by Jorge de Montemayor called *Diana* a shepherd's love is changed by a charm.

6. The transformation of Bottom was also influenced by *The Golden Ass* and a similar occurrence in Reginald Scot's *Discouerie of Witchcraft* (1584).

7. Most of the fairy material is derived from English folklore. Puck is a typical example coming, no doubt, from fairy songs about Robin

Goodfellow (the two names are used interchangeably for the same spirit). The diminutive fairies were probably of Shakespeare's own invention.

ADDITIONAL NOTES

Date of the Play
The play was probably written in 1595 after *Richard II*. It was first printed in 1600.

The Structure
Main plot: the love affairs of Lysander, Hermia, Demetrius and Helena.

Sub-plots
  (i)   The Love affair of Theseus and Hippolyta and their marriage.
 (ii)   The activities of the artisans, leading up to their performance of 'Pyramus and Thisbe'.
(iii)   The quarrel of Oberon and Titania and the involvement of the fairies.

Music in the play
Shakespeare was not the first dramatist to introduce music in his plays. It was traditional for trumpet calls to be used – alarums, retreats, flourishes and other signals often appear in stage directions. Musicians were often brought on the stage to accompany the actors. In Shakespeare's plays generally, music served a number of purposes.
   (i)   It provided atmosphere.
  (ii)   It accentuated words already spoken by the actors. Thus the songs introduced at different intervals in the play reflect particular moods.
 (iii)   It filled pauses in the action.
  (iv)   It gave opportunities for the audience to think about what had already happened.
   (v)   It allowed time for explanations.
  (vi)   It served to express joyfulness at a happy event.
 (vii)   It provided variety for the audience.
(viii)   It provided opportunities for actor participation and perhaps audience participation.

In *A Midsummer Night's Dream* the songs make up an important part of the action. In Act II, Scene 2, for example, the song 'You spotted snakes with double tongue' is used as a device to make Titania fall asleep. The music adds to the fairy-like quality of the play. The main songs are:

– Over hill, over dale

(Act II, Scene 1)

– You spotted snakes with double tongue

(Act II, Scene 2)

– The ousel cock so black of hue

(Act III, Scene 1)

– Through the house give glimmering light

(Act V, Scene 1)

– Now until the break of day

(Act V, Scene 1)

The play's language and style

Throughout the play there is a preponderance of antithesis in the speeches of the characters, of figurative expressions, of classical allusions and there are frequent 'conceits' (puns). The emphasis throughout is upon incident rather than character and the play is more like a masque (a singing and dancing event) than a play. Prose is used as a general rule for comic exchange and for the dialogue of those in low social positions (i.e. the artisans). Blank verse is the main vehicle of expression while rhymed verse is used in the songs and at the end of the scenes. Much of the language is lyrical and much of the imagery is derived from the references to the moon, the stars and night-time when fairies reputedly abound.

Classical imagery in the play

The play is set in ancient Athens and thus, throughout, there are numerous allusions to mythology. The chief of these are given below.

ACT 1

Amazons – a belligerent race of women near the Bosphorus. Their queen was Hippolyta, captured and imprisoned by Theseus.

Diana – the Roman goddess of chastity, hunting and the moon, and daughter of Zeus.

Golden head – a reference to the arrows of Cupid. Those with gold tips induced love and those with lead, hate.

Venus' doves – doves were birds symbolic of innocence and purity. They were sacred to Venus, the Roman goddess of love.

The Carthage Queen – this is a reference to Dido, the queen of Carthage, who fell in love with the Trojan Aeneas. When he sailed away without returning her love she built a funeral pyre and threw herself on it.

The false Trojan – Aeneas. See story above.

Phoebe – another name for Diana.

Cupid – the Roman god of love, represented as a winged boy with a bow and arrow. He was the son of Mars and Venus and his Greek counterpart is Eros.

Phibbus' car – the chariot of Phoebus, the Greek god of the sun.

Ercles' vein – Hercules was a hero remembered for his great strength and courage. Thus 'Ercles vein' means in the way that Hercules would do something.

Thisby's Mother – Pyramus and Thisbe were two famous lovers in Greek legend living in Babylon. Pyramus, wrongly thinking Thisbe was dead killed himself. Thisbe encountering him in his death throes, killed herself.

ACT II

Corin) – traditional names for bucolic lovers
Phillida) – in pastoral poetry.

Amazon – a reference to Hippolyta, Queen of the Amazons.

Perigenia – an early love of Theseus, the daughter of an enemy he killed.

Aegles – another early love of Theseus.

Ariadne – another early love of Theseus. He deserted Aegles for her. All three loves above – Perigenia, Aegles and Ariadne – were all mentioned as former loves of Theseus in Plutarch's *Lives*.

Antiopa – an Amazon prisoner of Theseus.

Hiems – the Latin word for winter. (Winter is personified).

Neptune – the Roman God of the Sea, the son of Cronos and Rhea.

Apollo – the Greek god of light, poetry, music, healing and prophecy and the epitome of ideal manhood.

Daphne – a beautiful nymph who disliked the amorous attentions of Apollo. She tried to escape from him and asked the gods for help. She was turned by them into a laurel tree which became Apollo's favourite tree.

Philomel – in Greek mythology she was turned from a woman into a bird (a nightingale).

ACT III

Her brother's noontide – 'Her' refers to the goddess Diana. Her brother was Apollo, the god of the sun, hence 'noontide'.

Ninus – the founder of Nineveh and the husband of the famous builder of Babylon where Thisbe and Pyramus lived.

Venus – the Roman goddess of love (Greek counterpart – Aphrodite) and daughter of Jupiter.

Tartars – a race of invading marauders who were famous as archers.

Taurus – a mountain range in Turkey.

Acheron – one of the four rivers of Hell.

Aurora's harbinger – the morning star, forerunner of Aurora, the goddess of the rising sun (the dawn).

the morning's love – Cephalus, the hunter, was wooed by Aurora but remained faithful to his wife Procris.

ACT IV

Dian's bud – a herb reputed to promote chastity. Diana was the Roman goddess of chastity.

Cadmus – son of the King of Phoenicia and sower of truth from which armed men, Sparti, arose.

Sparta – a city-state near Greece and famous for its dogs.

Thessalian bulls – hunting bulls on horseback was a predilection of the Thessalians who were of Greek nationality.

ACT V

The Battle with the Centaurs – a Centaur was one of a race of creatures with the head, arms and torso of a man, and the lower body and legs of a horse.

Thebes – an ancient Greek city, arch enemy of Athens.

Bacchanals – followers of Bacchus, the Greek god of wine.

The Tracian Singer – a reference to Orpheus a famous poet and musician (lyre player) of Greek mythology. He married Eurydice and sought her in Hades when she died. He failed to get her back and was eventually killed by the Thracian women.

Limander – a reference to Leander who in Greek legend was a youth from Abydos. He drowned in the Hellespont in a storm on one of his nightly visits to Hero, his loved one.

Muses – the nine sister goddesses each of whom was regarded as the protectress of a different art or science. They were the daughters of Zeus and Mnemosyne and the nine were Calliope, Clio, Erato, Euterpe, Melpomene, Polyhymnia, Terpischore, Thalia and Urania.

Shafalus to Procrus – see the reference to the morning's love (under Act III). Cephalus was wooed by Aurora but remained true to his wife Procris. Not trusting him, Procris followed him to see what his reactions to Aurora were. Cephalus thought the noises Procris made as she hid were made by a dangerous animal and he killed her by accident.

Furies – daughters of the Night who carried out the vengeance of the gods.

Fates – there were three of these said to control human lives. Clotho held the spindle of birth, Lachesis spun life's thread and Atropos (reputed to be blind) cut the thread with the scissors of death.

Triple Hecate's team – the Greek goddess Hecate ruled over heaven, earth and Hell.

their issue – a reference to the child of Theseus and Hippolyta, named Hippolytus. He was killed after his stepmother falsely accused him of raping her.

LEARNING QUOTATIONS

Quotations are an important part of an essay. It is pointless, however, to quote passages which do not illustrate the point that you are trying to make.

One way of deciding which quotations to learn is to distinguish important themes and subjects in the work that you are studying. These are likely to be the topics on which you are examined, so you will be prepared with some quotations to use in your essays.

Suggested quotations for committing to memory are arranged below under heading of major themes (not exhaustive).

A Midsummer Night's Dream is much concerned with ideas of contrast. Between disorder and harmony, dream and reality, love and hate, town and country – the play (a) explores how far these are real opposites and finds that some are not and (b) unites differences that do exist in a balanced harmony. The essence of this process is expressed in Hippolytas' words about the baying of the hounds – all separately make a different noise but blend into a harmonious whole:

Act IV Scene 1   Lines 113-117
HIPPOLYTA

               Never did I hear

to   So musical a discord, such sweet thunder.

The main speech on disorder occurs in Act II Scene 1   Lines 81-117 (or parts of)
TITANIA

        These are the forgeries of jealousy;

to   We are their parents and original.

Act III Scene 2   Lines 162-167
LYSANDER

        You are unkind, Demetrius. Be not so,

to   Whom I do love, and will do to my death.

Lines 169-173

DEMETRIUS

        Lysander, keep thy Hermia. I will none.

to   There to remain.

Act IV Scene 1   Lines 163-175
DEMETRIUS

        But, my good lord – I wot not by what power,

to   And will for evermore be true to it.

Act III Scene 2   Lines 458-463

PUCK

       And the country proverb known,

to   The man shall have his mare again, and all shall be well.

2. There are numerous references to dreams and dreaming, some of the main ones are as follows:

Act I Scene 1   Lines 6-7

HIPPOLYTA

       Four days will quickly steep themselves in night;

to   Of our solemnities.

Act III Scene 2   Lines 370-373

OBERON

       When they next wake, all this derision

to   With league whose date till death shall never end.

Act IV Scene 1   Lines 74-75

TITANIA

       My Oberon, what visions I have seen!

to   Methought I was enamoured of an ass.

Act IV Scene 1   Lines 145-147

LYSANDER

       My lord, I shall reply amazedly,

to   I cannot truly say how I came here.

Lines 186-187

DEMETRIUS

       These things seem small and undistinguishable,

to   Like far-off mountains turnéd into clouds.

and   Lines 192-194

       Are you sure

to   That yet we sleep, we dream.

Lines 203-216

BOTTOM

       I have had a most rare vision . . . . .

to   . . . . . .I shall sing it at her death.

Act V Scene 1   Lines 413-420
> PUCK
>
> > If we shadows have offended,
> to   If you pardon, we will mend.

3. Contrast between mature love affair of Theseus and Hippolyta and the quarrels and indecision of Lysander, Hermia, Demetrius and Helena.

Act I Scene 1   Lines 12-19
> THESEUS
>
> > Go, Philostrate,
> to   With pomp, with triumph, and with revelling.
>   and   Lines 124-126
> > I must employ you in some business
> to   Of something nearly that concerns yourselves.

Act I Scene 1   Lines 188-193
> HELENA
>
> > My ear should catch your voice, my eye your eye,
> to   You sway the motion of Demetrius' heart.

Act II Scene 2   Lines 117-122
> LYSANDER
>
> > Content with Hermia? No, I do repent
> to   And reason says you are the worthier maid.

Act III Scene 2   Lines 271-277
> HERMIA
>
> > What? Can you do me greater harm than hate?
> to   In earnest, shall I say?
> and   Lines 110-115
> PUCK
>
> > Captain of our fairy band,
> to   Lord, what fools these mortals be!
> and   Lines 118-121
> PUCK
>
> > Then will two at once woo one –
> to   That befall preposterously.

4. The connection between Oberon and Titania's love and that of Theseus and Hippolyta.

Act II Scene 1   Lines 64-73

TITANIA

      . . . . . .But I know

to   To give their bed joy and prosperity.

Lines 74-80

OBERON

      How canst thou thus, for shame, Titania,

to   With Ariadne, and Antiopa?

Act IV Scene 1   Lines 84-91

OBERON

      Sound, music! (*Music*) Come, my Queen, take hands with me

to   Wedded with Theseus all in jollity.

5. Contrasting types of humour: lords and ladies puns and wit, 'the mechanicals' situation comedy and humour in their verbal mistakes.

Act V Scene 1   Lines 299-302

DEMETRIUS

      No die, but an ace for him; for he is but one.

to   THESEUS

      With the help of a surgeon he might yet recover, and prove an ass.

Act III Scene 1   Lines 53-58

QUINCE

      Ay; or else one must come in . . . . . .

to   . . . . . . did talk through the chink of a wall

Lines 112-115

BOTTOM

      I see their knavery!

to   . . . . . . I am not afraid.

6. Oberon's speeches are much quoted to illustrate their poetic imagery.

Act II Scene 1   Lines 148-154

OBERON

      My gentle Puck, come hither. Thou rememberest

to   To hear the sea-maid's music?

and   Lines 249-258

      I know a bank where the wild thyme blows,

to   And make her full of hateful fantasies.

MODEL ANSWERS
O LEVEL STANDARD

CONTENTS

1. How many different stories are told in *A Midsummer Night's Dream?* State briefly what they are and how they are interwoven. (O)

Five stories are related in *A Midsummer Night's Dream.* The story to which the audience is first introduced is that of Theseus's wedding to Hippolyta, and it is this story which serves as a framework for everything else in the play. At the beginning of the first Act, Theseus tells Hippolyta:

> our nuptial hour
> Draws on apace.

(Act I, Scene 1)

In the time which intervenes between the first scene and the 'nuptial' hour, the main action of the play takes place. As well as providing a framework for the other stories, that of Theseus and Hippolyta is interwoven with the others, and helps to bring them to a happy conclusion, for Theseus uses his position to bring about happy marriages for the other lovers and to enable the Athenian craftsmen to fulfil their ambition by giving permission to allow them to perform their play.

The second story concerns the young lovers: Hermia, Lysander, Helena and Demetrius. The difficulties for these lovers begin in the first scene of the play when Egeus opposes the desire of his daughter, Hermia, to marry Lysander. Later, in Acts II and III, the concerns of the lovers are interwoven with, and directly affected by, the actions of the fairies. Puck is the principal link between the lovers and the fairy world. It is he who says of Lysander, in Act II, Scene 2:

> Weeds of Athens he doth wear

and who therefore makes the mistake of putting the magic juice on the wrong man's eyes. Oberon eventually corrects the mistake and in Act IV, Scene 1, Theseus brings the story to a happy conclusion:

> Egeus, I will overbear your will;
> For in the temple by and by with us
> These couples shall eternally be knit.

(Act IV, Scene 1)

The third story concerns the quarrel between Oberon and Titania. We first learn of this from Puck, in Act II, Scene 1. Oberon is annoyed because Titania has in her service:

> a changeling,
> And jealous Oberon would have the child
> Knight of his train . . . .

(Act II, Scene 1)

Later the King and Queen of the fairies meet and quarrel, accusing each other of infidelity as well as arguing over the changeling boy. The story of how Oberon eventually wins the boy is interwoven with the story of human lovers, and also provides an amusing complement to the other tales in *A Midsummer Night's Dream* of difficulties encountered in love.

The fourth story concerns the efforts at drama of Quince, Bottom and their friends. We meet them first in Act II, Scene 1, even before the first appearance of the fairies. They appear again in Act III, Scene 1, rehearsing in the wood, and in Act IV, Scene 2, when they are reunited and Bottom announces: 'our play is preferred'. Finally they appear before the Duke in Act V, Scene 1. The fact that Bottom is given an ass's head by Puck and is loved by Titania provides a further link with other stories in the play.

The fifth and final story is that which is clumsily related by the Athenian craftsmen, namely the 'very tragical mirth' of 'Pyramus and Thisbe'. This fits perfectly into the overall pattern of *A Midsummer Night's Dream* because it is, taken seriously, yet another story illustrating the fact that:

> The course of true love never did run smooth
>
> (Act I, Scene 1)

and is the other side of the coin to the comedy, the tragedy that could have been made out of the same facts handled differently. Moreover, it provides some amusing moments at the time when all the lovers in *A Midsummer Night's Dream* are happily united. Their delight in watching it symbolises their joy at this time.

The last Act of the play brings all five of the stories to a happy conclusion. Theseus and Hippolyta are married, the lovers get the partners they want, the Athenian craftsmen have their moment of triumph, Theseus declaring that 'Pyramus and Thisbe':

> hath well beguiled
> The heavy gait of night
>
> (Act V, Scene 1)

and Titania and Oberon are reunited, to dance, sing and bless the newlyweds.

2. Give an account, in the correct order, of the actions of Helena in *A Midsummer Night's Dream*. *(O)*

We learn from Lysander, early in the first scene of the play, that Helena had been loved by Demetrius, who 'won her soul' (Act I, Scene 1).

It is not surprising, then, that when she first appears, in Act I, Scene 1 she is dejected and envies Hermia's charms, which have stolen Demetrius' heart.

Hermia comforts her, by telling her that she plans to elope with Lysander and is not interested in Demetrius. Helena, left alone, decides to pass this news on to Demetrius, in the pathetic hope that he will thank her for the information and might love her for her unselfishness.

When Helena next appears, in Act II, Scene 1, she is with Demetrius in the wood, seeking Lysander and Hermia. Demetrius scorns her and urges her not to pursue him, but she is content to be his 'spaniel'. When he runs away from her, she follows faithfully, willing, if necessary:

> To die upon the hand I love so well.
>
> (Act II, Scene 1)

Before Helena appears again, in Act II, Scene 2, a good deal happens. Lysander's eyes are anointed with the love juice which will make him love the first person he sees, and he is asleep on the stage. Helena is exhausted with pursuing Demetrius and she is very miserable:

> For beasts that meet me run away for fear.
>
> (Act II, Scene 2)

Lysander awakes and instantly loves her. She regards his declarations of love as 'mockery' and runs away. He deserts Hermia and pursues Helena.

In Act III, Scene 2, Lysander has caught up with her and continues to declare his love, but they have come upon the sleeping Demetrius, whose eyes, by now, are also anointed with the potion. He awakes and declares his love. However, Helena believes that he, too, is mocking her with a pretence of love:

> O spite! O hell! I see you are all bent
> To set against me for your merriment
>
> (Act III, Scene 2)

When Hermia also arrives, the situation is very confused. Helena assumes that Hermia is also: 'one of this confederacy'. (Act III, Scene 2). She reminds Hermia of their life-long friendship and is furious that Hermia should:

> join with men in scorning your poor friend
>
> (Act III, Scene 2)

On her side, Hermia at first cannot understand Lysander's behaviour, but at last becomes convinced that he really loves Helena. Thinking that Helena has stolen Lysander's love, she attacks not Lysander but poor Helena herself. The resulting quarrel has some amusing moments. Helena's part in it includes an insult to Hermia's lack of height:

> you counterfeit, you puppet, you!
>
> (Act III, Scene 2)

and a plea to the men to defend her. She confesses to Hermia that she told Demetrius of the planned elopement. Later, after she warns the men of Hermia's temper:

> She was a vixen when she went to school,
>
> (Act III, Scene 2)

they both take her part against Hermia. Eventually, left alone with Hermia, Helena uses her long legs to run away.

At the end of Act III, Scene 2, Helena, exhausted, and intending to return to Athens by daylight, falls asleep in the wood. While the lovers sleep, Puck, on Oberon's orders, squeezes the other magic juice into Lysander's eyes. As a result, when the lovers are awakened by Theseus, in Act IV, Scene 1, problems are resolved. Only Demetrius loves Helena, and she accepts his love with hardly any misgivings:

> And I have found Demetrius like a jewel,
>
> Mine own and not mine own.
>
> (Act IV, Scene 1)

Finally, Helena, now married to Demetrius, appears with all the other newly-weds in Act V, Scene 1. Like Hermia, she does not speak again, but she is a member of the delighted audience of 'Pyramus and Thisbe'.

3. What do you find amusing about the behaviour of Bottom, during the first meeting of the Athenian craftsmen, at Peter Quince's house? (O)

During the first meeting of the Athenian craftsmen, at Quince's house, in Act I, Scene 2, the amusing aspects of Bottom's behaviour stem from the incongruity between the high opinion Bottom has of himself and the opinion of him rapidly formed by the audience. He obviously regards himself as well-qualified to lead and instruct the others. He urges Quince to call the roll, 'man by man', to make sure all are present. However, as there are only six men involved, this hardly seems necessary. Later, hearing that the play is to be about 'Pyramus and Thisbe', he says: 'A very good piece of work, I assure you, and a merry.' However, only a few moments later, his words prove that in fact he knows nothing about the play: 'What is Pyramus? – a lover or a tyrant?' His ignorance, coupled with self-assurance, is amusingly exposed, too, in his presumptious requests to play the parts of Thisbe and the Lion as well as his own. The audience laughs because he is so conceited that he really believes himself a fine actor: 'That will ask some tears in the true performing of it. If I do it, let the audience look to their eyes! I will move storms. I will condole, in some measure.' He is so proud of his own brilliance that he keeps on interrupting poor Quince, in order to impress the company with his talents. Like the others, he is naïve enough to believe that the ladies at court will be frightened by the Lion's roar if it is too loud.

Another cause of amusement in Bottom's behaviour concerns the use of his voice when he tries to impress his friends with his acting skills. His pompous recitation in 'Ercles' vein' or the 'monstrous little voice' he uses to impersonate Thisbe are bound to evoke laughter from any audience.

His behaviour is amusing, too, because it shows that he is susceptible to flattery. He wants to play three parts, but Quince knows how to cajole and flatter him into confining himself to the role of Pyramus: 'Pyramus is a sweet-faced man; a proper man as one shall see in a summer's day...' Bottom yields to the flattery, agrees to undertake the part, and at once becomes distracted about the selection of an appropriate beard.

Moreover, Bottom's behaviour amuses because he uses words in a way which also reveals ignorance coupled with unbounded self-assurance. He will use a 'monstrous' little voice; he speaks of 'Thisbe'; he can 'aggravate' his voice, and he tells the actors that, in the wood, they will be able to rehearse 'most obscenely'.

To sum up, the behaviour of Bottom, who dominates this scene, is amusing because it shows him to be a simple, ignorant workman whose opinion of his own abilities is much higher than it should be. This is apparent from Bottom's ignorance as he sets out to lead the others, his mistaken ideas about good acting, his susceptibility to flattery and his misuse of words.

4. What is the attitude of Theseus to (a) Hermia, (b) Lysander, and (c) Demetrius? (O)

(a) To Hermia, Theseus is kind and sympathetic, but because it is his duty to administer the Athenian law, and because he respects her father, Egeus, he deals firmly with her.

After hearing the plea of Egeus, in Act I Scene I, he politely advises (rather than orders) Hermia to obey her father's will:

> To you your father should be as a god;
> One that composed your beauties.
>
> (Act I, Scene 1)

He agrees that Lysander is a worthy gentleman but, since Lysander lacks the approval of Egeus, he urges her to marry Demetrius. When she refuses, he is obliged to give his judgement and in this matter he is more kind than Hermia's own father, for he does not force Hermia to choose between Demetrius and death but gives her the additional choice of becoming a nun. Moreover, he gives her four days in which to reach her decision.

Theseus also knows that Demetrius has proved an inconstant lover and this no doubt influences his attitude to Hermia. It is not surprising that, when Demetrius returns to Helena, Theseus sensibly says:

> Egeus, I will overbear your will.

> (Act IV, Scene 1)

(b) To Lysander, Theseus is as kind and fair as he is permitted to be within the limits of Athenian law. He agrees with Hermia that Lysander: 'In himself' (Act I, Scene 1) is a worthy man, but insists that, because Lysander lacks Egeus' approval, Demetrius must be regarded as worthier. When Lysander, in his own defence, points out that Demetrius has jilted the unhappy Helena, Theseus says:

> I must confess that I have heard so much.

> (Act I, Scene 1)

and his remark that he intended to speak with Demetrius on the matter proves that he sympathises with Lysander and acknowledges that the young man has just cause for complaint. For the moment, though, he feels obliged to administer the law strictly, unpleasant though this may be.

However, his kindness to Lysander in Act IV, Scene I, makes admirable redress for the pain the young man suffered earlier. Strictly speaking, Lysander should now lose Hermia to Demetrius and should also be punished for the crime, to which he confesses, of having eloped with Hermia. But after hearing the confession, and the speeches of Egeus and Demetrius, Theseus gives his judgement in favour of the lovers:

> For in the temple by and by with us
> These couples shall eternally be knit.

> (Act IV, Scene 1)

(c) The attitude of Theseus to Demetrius is different from his attitude to Hermia and Lysander. With them he feels sympathy, though the law obliges him to be hard on them; with Demetrius, he feels less sympathy, though the law obliges the Duke to be kind to him.

In Act I, Scene 1, he supports Demetrius only because this young man has the approval of Hermia's father. He knows, however, that Demetrius has jilted Helena:

> I must confess that I have heard so much,
> And with Demetrius thought to have spoke thereof
> But, being overfull of self-affairs,
> My mind did lose it.

> (Act I, Scene 1)

Even now, he takes Demetrius and Egeus away for some: 'private schooling' (Act I, Scene 1)

In view of what happens in this first scene, it is obvious that he will be delighted if Demetrius returns to Helena, and when he finds that this has happened, in Act IV, Scene 1, he immediately arranges the triple wedding, allowing Egeus no further opportunity for support from the law.

5. What are (a) the causes and (b) the effects of the quarrel between Oberon and Titania? (0)

(a) The most important cause of the quarrel between Oberon and Titania concerns a changeling boy. Titania has;

> A lovely boy stolen from an Indian king

(Act II, Scene 1)

but Oberon, who is jealous:

> would have the child
> Knight of his train, to trace the forests wild.

(Act II, Scene 1)

Titania, however, refused to surrender the boy to her husband. She determines to keep him because the boy's mother was a 'votaress' of her order, who served her well. Moreover, when the mother died, giving birth to the boy, Titania decided to care for the infant. She says:

> And for her sake do I rear up her boy;
> And for her sake I will not part with him.

(Act II, Scene 1)

Another cause of the quarrel is that they are jealous of each other's love of mortals. Titania accuses Oberon of loving Hippolyta. He accuses Titania of loving Theseus. These accusations, however, 'the forgeries of jealousy, (Act II, Scene 1) are probably made in the heat of their tempers, and are only symptoms of the more serious quarrel involving the changeling boy.

(b) The quarrel has several effects. The first concerns Nature, with direct, unpleasant results for mortals. The winds, 'piping' in vain to Titania and Oberon, take revenge by sucking up, from the sea, water in the form of fogs. The fogs then fall on the land, causing floods.

> The ox hath therefore stretched his yoke in vain,
> The ploughman lost his sweat, and the green corn
> Hath rotted ere his youth attained a beard.

(Act II, Scene 1)

Village games are spoiled The animals are afflicted with disease. The moon is angry, too, and

> washes all the air,
> That rheumatic diseases do abound

(Act II, Scene 1)

43

The quarrel also causes a disturbance in the seasons, and 'sweet summer buds' are covered by frost.

The quarrel affects the fairies and their revelry, too. For example, when Oberon and Titania argue,

> all their elves for fear
> Creep into acorn-cups and hide them there.
>
> (Act II, Scene 1)

Finally, the quarrel has effects on the plots of some of the stories told in *A Midsummer Night's Dream.* Because of it, Oberon first thinks of the 'little western flower' (Act II, Scene I) with which he later charms the eyes of Titania. Consequently, she falls in love with Bottom. Oberon also uses the herb with the kind intention of assisting the lovers, though with unsuccessful results at first.

6. From each of five different scenes give an example of an occasion when the audience could be expected to laugh. For each example, show clearly what causes the amusement. **(O)**

(i) In Act II, Scene 2, the audience could be expected to laugh at the point when Lysander, waking from his sleep, sees Helena and says at once:

> And run through fire I will for they sweet sake!
> Transparent Helena! Nature shows art,
> That through thy bosom makes me see thy heart.
>
> (Act II, Scene 2)

The amusement here is caused by the fact that Lysander, who has been so devoted to Hermia, now suddenly declares his love for Helena. Dramatic irony, as well as absurdity, makes this laughable, because the audience knows that Puck, making a mistake, has put the magic juice on Lysander's eyes.

(ii) The audience frequently laughs at misuses of words by the Athenian craftsmen, particularly Bottom. An example of this, from Act III, Scene 1, occurs at the moment when Bottom, saying that the actor playing the Lion must speak through the Lion's neck, makes the comment: 'and he himself must speak through, saying thus, or to the same defect . . .' Obviously Bottom should say 'effect' and not 'defect'. The audience laughs because the word 'defect' means 'fault' and makes us think that, as the play 'Pyramus and Thisbe' is so full of faults, 'defect' is perhaps not so inappropriate after all!

(iii) In Act III Scene 2 there is some amusing abuse hurled between Hermia and Helena. Both the women are upset; Hermia because she has become convinced that Helena has stolen her lover Lysander and Helena because she thinks Hermia has invented the accusation to join in the men's 'joke'. Rather than shout at the real culprit, Lysander, Hermia turns on Helena:

> And are you grown so high in his esteem
> Because I am so dwarfish and so low?
> How low am I, thou painted maypole? Speak!
> How low am I? – I am not yet so low
> But that my nails can reach unto thine eyes.

The lines are sarcastic, Hermia has invented an excuse to accuse Helena of abusing her by latching on to the word 'low' and taking it as an insult. In the usual way of quarrels, she then declares herself pleased to be small, Helena in contrast is a 'painted maypole' (quite a comical image is conjured up in this expression), and Hermia is tall enough for her needs i.e. to scratch out her eyes. Hermia's words are witty in themselves but much of the humour is in their vehemence, she has dropped any pretence of logical argument and resorted to simple abuse.

Helena defends herself by returning insult for insult. She makes fun of Hermia's lack of height by calling her a 'puppet'. Hermia returns the scorn, by describing Helena as a 'painted maypole'. The ladies' fury grows and it is left to the men to prevent them from fighting.

At last the men set off for their duel and Helena escapes from Hermia. Puck says:

> And so far am I glad it so did sort
> As this their jangling I esteem a sport.

(Act III, Scene 2)

However, he and Oberon now rectify their mistakes, and no lasting harm is done to the lovers.

(iv) In Act IV, Scene 2, when the Athenian craftsmen meet for the last time before their final production, the audience could be expected to laugh when Bottom says: 'And most dear actors, eat no onions nor garlic, for we are to utter sweet breath'. (Act IV, Scene 2). This is amusing because the fact that Bottom considers it necessary to give this advice implies that the craftsmen would not usually consider it unsociable to eat onions or garlic, and that it is quite normal for them not to have sweet-smelling breath.

(v) Finally, in the presentation of 'Pyramus and Thisbe' there are many occasions when the audience might be expected to laugh. An example, from Quince's prologue, is:

> Our true intent is. All for your delight
> We are not here. That you should here repent you . . . .

> (Act V, Scene 1)

The audience laughs because, by failing to give proper attention to the punctuation, Quince says almost the opposite to what he means. He should say:

> Our true intent is all for your delight.
> We are not here that you should here repent you. . . .

7. Summarise the actions of Demetrius in *A Midsummer Night's Dream*. (O)

At the beginning of the play, Demetrius is presented to the Duke as the man who has Egeus' approval to marry Hermia. However, Lysander considers Demetrius to be a 'spotted and inconstant man' (Act I, Scene 1) since he has loved and then deserted Helena, who is now obsessively in love with him.

Demetrius himself speaks only once in the first scene of the play, urging Lysander to relinquish any claim to Hermia. However, before he next appears, in Act II, Scene 1, Demetrius has been informed by Helena of the intended elopement of Lysander and Hermia and has come to the wood in pursuit of them. Helena, hoping to win favour, faithfully follows him, but he spurns her, urges her to leave him, and even says unkindly:

> Tempt not too much the hatred of my spirit;
> For I am sick when I do look on thee.

> (Act II, Scene 1)

Eventually, he runs away from her. In Act II, Scene 2, Helena catches him but he again escapes, leaving her exhausted. As a result she sleeps near Lysander, whose eyes have been anointed by Puck so that when he awakes, he instantly loves Helena.

In Act III, Scene 2, Demetrius at last finds Hermia and declares his love for her, only to be accused of having murdered Lysander. Demetrius feels too tired to go on in pursuit of Hermia and sleeps on the ground, where his eyes are anointed by Oberon. A few moments later, he wakes to see Helena and falls in love with her:

> O Helen, goddess, nymph, perfect, divine

> (Act III, Scene 2)

Both men now love Helena, and the misunderstandings and quarrel which result are very amusing. Demetrius' part, inevitably, is to urge Lysander to love Hermia:

> Lysander, keep thy Hermia. I will none.
> If e'er I loved her all that love is gone.

> (Act III, Scene 2)

46

When he fails to persuade by words, he decides to resort to force, and agrees to a duel with Lysander. Before the men set off, however, Demetrius sarcastically insults Lysander for being held by a 'weak' bond, namely Hermia's arms. He stays with Lysander, hearing the ladies' quarrel, and, like Lysander, he offers to defend Helena. Finally, the men set off to fight, but Oberon and Puck intervene to prevent actual bloodshed. Puck, imitating the voice of one, then of the other, leads them apart in the dark. Demetrius, believing Lysander is running away like a coward, eventually has to sleep, but is determined to seek his adversary in the morning.

In Act IV, Scene 1, when Theseus wakes all the lovers, Lysander having been anointed with the antidote, once more loves Hermia. Demetrius announces his love for Helena, and the Duke immediately arranges the weddings the lovers desire. There are no more thoughts about the duel. Demetrius thinks he has been dreaming:

> These things seem small and undistinguishable,
> Like far-off mountains turned into clouds.
>
> (Act IV, Scene 1)

In the final scene, Demetrius is a member of the audience watching 'Pyramus and Thisbe' and contributes to the comments on it. It is he, for example, who says of the pieces of apparatus carried by Moonshine:

> Why, all these should be in the lantern; for all these
> are in the moon.
>
> (Act V, Scene 1)

Finally, after watching the Bergomask dance, he leaves, together with his wife, Helena, and all the other courtiers.

8. What do we learn of Puck's mischievousness? (O)

In Act II, Scene 1, when Puck first appears, the Fairy identifies him as:

> that shrewd and knavish sprite
> Called Robin Goodfellow.

It is he, she says:

> That frights the maidens of the villagery,
> Skim milk, and sometimes labour in the quern,
> And bootless make the breathless housewife churn,
> And sometime make the drink to bear no barm . . . .
>
> (Act II, Scene 1)

In addition to interfering with housewives' work, he also leads wanderers astray in the dark and laughs at their confusion.

Puck admits all this and tells the Fairy that he also amuses Oberon with such pranks as teasing horses, or hiding in an old lady's bowl, in the form of a crab-apple:

And when she drinks, against her lips I bob
And on her withered dewlap pour the ale.

(Act II, Scene 1)

Sometimes he assumes the shape of a three-legged stool and when a lady, telling a solemn tale, sits on him, he slips from under her so that she falls down.

Puck's delight in tormenting people is obvious later, too, when he relates to Oberon how he interfered with the rehearsal of 'Pyramus and Thisbe'. Not only did he enjoy fixing an ass's head on Bottom, but he was also delighted by the terror this inspired in Bottom's companions. They ran off, crying 'murder' and screaming for help. They tore their clothes on briars and thorns, and, Puck mischievously adds:

I led them on in this distracted fear,
And left sweet Pyramus translated there.

(Act III, Scene 2)

Later in this scene, when it has been discovered that he made a mistake with the love juice, Puck enjoys the 'sport' resulting from the confusion he has caused:

And those things do best please me
That befall preposterously.

(Act III, Scene 2)

After observing with Oberon the resulting quarrels, Puck still says, remorselessly:

And so far am I glad it so did sort,
As this their jangling I esteem a sport.

(Act III, Scene 2)

This is another example of his characteristic delight at the plight of people he has himself misled.

When we see Puck behaving mischievously for the last time, he is, on Oberon's instructions, leading Demetrius and Lysander apart. With obvious delight he imitates the voices, first of the one, then of the other.

Although Puck is full of mischief and laughs at those whom he misleads, he is kind and helpful to some people, namely those who call him 'Hobgoblin' and 'Sweet Puck'. As the Fairy says to him:

You do their work, and they shall have good luck.

(Act II, Scene 1)

9. Summarise briefly what you associate with: (a) 'Your spaniel' (b) 'this confederacy' (c) 'Cupid's fiery shaft.' **(O)**

(a) Helena sees herself as the spaniel of Demetrius, when she says in Act II, Scene 1:

> I am your spaniel; and, Demetrius,
> The more you beat me I will fawn on you.
> Use me but as your spaniel: spurn me, strike me,
> Neglect me, lose me; only give me leave,
> Unworthy as I am, to follow you.

It is particularly appropriate that she sees herself as a spaniel, since spaniels have long been noted for their patient devotion even when they are ill-treated by their masters. Demetrius is treating her harshly in this scene: she has informed him of the elopement of Lysander and Hermia, and, for her pains, he merely tells her he does not love her and urges her not to follow him.

(b) The expression 'this confederacy' is used by Helena in Act III, Scene 2, when she says of Hermia:

> Lo, she is one of this confederacy.

She means that Hermia is taking part, with Lysander and Demetrius, in a cruel plot to mock her because Lysander, whom she knows to love Hermia, has now declared his love for Helena. Hermia herself seems to be joining in with the cruel joke by pretending to be angry at Lysander's words.

In fact, there is no confederacy at all. Unknown to the young people, Lysander's eyes have been anointed with the magic juice. The result is that Lysander really does love Helena at this moment.

(c) The expression 'Cupid's fiery shaft' occurs in a speech by Oberon to Puck in Act II, Scene 1. He tells Puck that on one occasion, he saw Cupid flying, armed:

> between the cold moon and the earth

He took aim at a certain fair maiden, but he missed, for Oberon saw:

> Cupid's fiery shaft
> Quenched in the chaste beams of the watery moon.

The arrow fell on a certain flower – 'love in idleness', the pansy. As a result, the flower turned from white to purple and received a magic power: when its juice is placed on the eyes of a sleeper and the person wakes, he or she falls passionately in love with 'the next live creature that it sees'.

Puck is sent to fetch the flower. Its juice is used subsequently on the eyes of Titania, Lysander and Demetrius, with considerable effects on later incidents.

The fact that Cupid's fiery shaft was once seen by Oberon to miss its mark is clearly of great importance to the stories interwoven in *A Midsummer Night's Dream*.

10. On what occasions do Lysander and Demetrius change their affections? How do they account for these changes? (O)

In Act I, Scene 1, Lysander is established as Hermia's lover. The first change in Lysander's affections occurs in Act II, Scene 2, after his eyes have been anointed mistakenly, by Puck. He awakes and immediately sees Helena, and under the effect of the potion falls in love with her. He says to her:

> Nature shows art
> That through thy bosom makes me see thy heart.
>
> (Act II, Scene 2)

To explain his change of affection, he says:

> Who will not change a raven for a dove?
> The will of man is by his reason swayed,
> And reason says you are the worthier maid.
>
> (Act II, Scene 2)

'Reason', then, has led him to love Helena, and he explains that, in earlier years, his reason was insufficiently developed for him to recognise her merits.

In Act III, Scene 2, Lysander continues to argue on these lines. He says of Hermia:

> I had no judgement when to her I swore.
>
> (Act III, Scene 2)

The second change in Lysander's affection becomes apparent in Act IV, Scene 1, after the second potion has been squeezed into his eyes by Puck. He awakes, confused, loving Hermia again. He does not account for his short-lived love for Helena, but says to Theseus:

> My lord, I shall reply amazedly,
> Half sleep, half waking.
>
> (Act IV, Scene 1)

His words imply that he now believes he has always really loved Hermia.

Demetrius loved Helena before he loved Hermia. He believes he has a:

> certain right
>
> (Act I, Scene 1)

to Hermia. He does not explain how his love for Helena has gone, but he says to her:

> I am sick when I do look on thee.
>
> (Act II, Scene 1)

Demetrius' affections change next after his eyes have been anointed by Puck (Act III, Scene 2). He awakes to see Helena. He loves her at once and explains the change of affection not in terms of reason, as Lysander did, but as the effect of her beauty:

> O, let me kiss
> This princess of pure white, this seal of bliss!

(Act III, Scene 2)

Of Hermia he says:

> My heart to her but as guestwise sojourned,
> And now to Helen is it home returned,
> There to remain.

(Act III, Scene 2)

Later, when Demetrius has to explain the new state of affairs to Theseus, he says:

> I wot not by what power –
> But by some power it is – my love to Hermia,
> Melted as the snow, seems to me now
> As the remembrance of an idle gaud,
> Which in my childhood I did dote upon.

(Act IV, Scene 1)

He goes on to compare himself and Helena with a sick man and his food. Just as the sick man loathes food, so he loathed Helena for a time. Now, however, he is 'in health' again, and returns to his 'natural taste', Helena.

11. **'My Oberon, what visions have I seen!**
Methought I was enamoured of an ass.'

(Act IV, Scene 1)

Give a full account of what had happened to Titania. **(O)**

Because Titania refused to give the changeling boy to Oberon, he decided to find a way of punishing her. He sent Puck to fetch the flower 'love in idleness', on which Cupid's dart had once fallen. He knew that if he put its juice on Titania's eyes:

> The next thing then she, waking, looks upon –
> Be it on lion, bear, or wolf, or bull,
> On meddling monkey, or on busy ape –
> She shall pursue it with the soul of love.

(Act II, Scene 1)

He would force her to surrender the child before releasing her from the charm by the application of another herb.

He himself anoints Titania's eyes with the juice, as she sleeps on a

> bank whereon the wild thyme blows,
> Where oxlips and the nodding violet grows

(Act II, Scene 1)

Many things happen before Titania wakes. In particular, the Athenian craftsmen have their rehearsal in which Puck mischievously intervenes, placing the ass's head on Bottom. Trying to give himself confidence by singing, Bottom awakens Titania, who loves his 'note' and even his 'shape'. She tells him:

51

> Thou shalt remain here, whether thou wilt or no.
> I am a spirit of no common rate.
> The summer still doth tend upon my state;
> And I do love thee.

(Act III, Scene 1)

She orders her fairies to attend to Bottom's needs:

> Feed him with apricocks and dewberries,
> With purple grapes, green figs, and mulberries;
> The honey-bags steal from the humble bees,
> And for night-tapers crop their waxen thighs.

(Act III, Scene 2)

She then conducts Bottom to her 'bower'. When Puck reports to Oberon that Titania loves an ass, the Fairy King is delighted.

In Act IV, Scene 1, Titania and her fairies entertain Bottom, though his tastes in music and food are hardly such as Titania would share. Offered music, he requests 'the tongs and the bones' and his preference in food is 'a bottle of hay'. Finally, Bottom sleeps in the arms of Titania, who says:

> the female ivy so
> Enrings the barky fingers of the elm.
> O, how I love thee! How I dote on thee!

(Act IV, Scene 1)

When she too sleeps, Oberon pities her, especially as she has meanwhile surrendered the changeling boy to him. He removes the spell and she wakes, amazed by her 'visions'. She now says of Bottom:

> O, how mine eyes do loathe his visage now!

(Act IV, Scene 1)

12. What do you learn about any two of the Athenian craftsmen, other than Quince and Bottom? (O)

Flute

Francis Flute is a bellows-mender. In the production of 'Pyramus and Thisbe', he plays Thisbe.

Like all the craftsmen he is enthusiastic about the proposed drama and the possible honour of performing before the Duke. Also, like the others, he is quite ignorant to begin with, of the story of Pyramus and Thisbe. When he is told which part he has to play, he says: 'What is Thisbe? – a wandering knight?' (Act I, Scene 2). Not surprisingly he objects to playing the part of a female character, but makes no further complaint when he is told he can play the part in a mask. He is, in fact, well cast as Thisbe, since he is probably less masculine in appearance than the others. As he is the youngest his beard is no obstacle at present: it is simply 'coming'. Moreover, unlike some of the others, he is reasonably good at learning his part and performing it confidently before the Duke. As he has a leading role, this is quite an important attribute.

One deduces that Flute is placid and shy. Although he speaks up when performing his role, he speaks only when he has to. He does not really argue when obliged to play a female part and he makes no comment when the others deliberate on the difficulties of presenting Moonshine, a Wall and a frightening Lion. He has very little idea of what is required of an actor, for, at the rehearsal, he speaks all his lines at once, 'cues and all', but he is quick to learn and acts well in the actual performance.

He has a great admiration for Bottom. It is he who says of Bottom: 'he hath simply the best wit of any handicraft man in Athens' (Act IV, Scene 2) and it is he, too, who is sure the Duke would have given Bottom sixpence a day for life for playing Pyramus.

Bearing in mind his shyness, his ability to learn his lines and the fact that he once corrects the misuse of a word ('paramour') by Quince, one deduces that, though he has a retiring nature, he is quite intelligent.

Snug

Snug is a joiner who is given the part of the Lion in 'Pyramus and Thisbe'.

He too, is a timid person, and less clever than most of the others. When he is allocated his part, he says: 'Have you the lion's part written? Pray you, if it be, give it me, for I am slow of study.' (Act I, Scene 2). Later, at the rehearsal, he says nothing. This, in itself, is significant, since he chooses to remain silent even when a subject which concerns him more than anyone else is discussed. Bottom, Snout and Quince between them discuss the problem of presenting a Lion 'among ladies' and determine that he shall speak a prologue. He presumably accepts willingly all that they suggest, because he believes they are more capable men than himself.

Like all the others, however, he is delighted about the prospect of playing before the Duke, and it is he, in Act IV, Scene 2, who brings the news of the triple marriage and says: 'If our sport had gone forward, we had all been made men.' At the performance of the play, he speaks his prologue of eight lines and is admired for his roars.

He is a good-hearted, simple fellow, capable of managing easy tasks, but respectful of what he regards as the superior talents of such men as Bottom and Quince.

13. Show how Shakespeare uses dramatic irony for comic effects in *A Midsummer Night's Dream*. (O)

Dramatic irony occurs when words spoken on the stage have more significance for the audience than for the characters in the play. For this to be possible, the audience has to know something which the characters are supposed not to know. In *A Midsummer Night's Dream*, the fun is frequently due to dramatic irony.

Most of the situations involving dramatic irony occur in connection with the application and effects of the love juice. First, Puck puts the juice on the eyes of the wrong man, Lysander saying:

> Weeds of Athens he doth wear.
> This is he....

(Act II, Scene 1)

The audience knows he is wrong and eagerly awaits the effects on Lysander's behaviour. He, awakened by Helena, is at once in love with her. Here, the audience knows the reason for the love, but Lysander does not. It is amusing to see him seek excuses for his change of affection: 'reason says you are the worthier maid.' (Act II, Scene 2).

A similar pattern of events occurs when Demetrius' eyes are anointed. Helena is also the first person he sees on awaking and so he falls in love with her. When Hermia arrives, the comedy due to dramatic irony is enriched further, since both the ladies believe at first that the men are making a mockery of Helena. In addition, Helena accuses Hermia of persuading the men to play the 'cruel joke' on her. As the women's tempers flare and the men prepare for a duel, the effects of dramatic irony have become quite complex.

Later in the play, when the effects of the love juice are removed from Lysander's eyes, dramatic irony is responsible for our amusement at his confusion when he awakes. He thinks he must have been dreaming about the changes in his feelings.

In the case of Titania, the love juice produces similar situations in which the fun is based on dramatic irony. Absurdity and dramatic irony are the basis of a good joke when she awakes and says of Bottom:

> What angel wakes me from my flowery bed?

(Act III, Scene 1)

Like Lysander, she is amazed by her memories of apparently having been in love with an ass.

With Bottom, too, Shakespeare bases many jokes on dramatic irony. Bottom does not know in what way exactly he is 'translated' and it is clearly amusing when he says such things as: 'What do you see? You see an ass head of your own, do you?' (Act III, Scene 1) and 'I see their knavery.' This is to make an ass of me.' (Act III, Scene 1).

To sum up, Shakespeare uses dramatic irony for many comic effects in *A Midsummer Night's Dream*. The dramatic irony occurs because the audience knows that certain characters have been affected by magical powers, while the characters concerned do not know it.

14. What is: (a) Theseus' opinion of poets?
(b) Puck's opinion of the Athenian craftsmen?
(c) Hippolyta's opinion of the barking of Spartan hounds? **(O)**

(a)   Theseus speaks of poets in Act IV, Scene 1, after disagreeing with Hippolyta about the truth of the account the lovers have given of their adventures. He does not believe the lovers since, in his opinion, lovers are like madmen and poets: all three let their imaginations run away with them. Of the poet, he says:

> The poet's eye, in a fine frenzy rolling,
> Doth glance from heaven to earth, from earth to heaven.
> And as imagination bodies forth
> The forms of things unknown, the poet's pen
> Turns them to shapes, and gives to airy nothing
> A local habitation and a name.

(Act V, Scene 1)

The conclusion of the whole speech is:

> How easy is a bush supposed a bear?

(Act V, Scene 1)

In short, poets use their imaginations too freely, making something out of nothing.

(b)   Puck encounters the craftsmen in Act III, Scene 1, when he describes them as 'hempen homespuns', i.e. uncouth men (dressed in homespun cloth of hemp).
He has no compunction about wrecking their rehearsal and proceeds to scare them mercilessly. When he reports to Oberon, he calls them:

> A crew of patches, rude mechanicals
> That work for bread upon Athenian stalls.

(Act III, Scene 2)

He describes Bottom as:

> The shallowest thickskin of that barren sort

(Act III, Scene 2)

and tells Oberon with delight of the ways in which he tormented the craftsmen.
Clearly, Puck's opinion is that the craftsmen are simpletons, and he regards them as choice victims for his mischievous pranks.

55

(c)   Hippolyta says, in Act IV, Scene 1, that she was once with Hercules and Cadmus:

> When in a wood of Crete they bayed the bear
> With hounds of Sparta.

She enjoyed the sport very much, for, paradoxically, she found the discordant barking of the hounds a delightful sound:

> Never did I hear
> Such gallant chiding, for, besides the groves,
> The skies, the fountains, every region near
> Seemed all one mutual cry. I never heard
> So musical a discord, such sweet thunder.

15. What are Helena's feelings about her own beauty?   (O)

Early in the play Helena is despondent about her own beauty and envious of Hermia's, which is so attractive to Demetrius:

> Demetrius loves your fair. O happy fair!
> Your eyes are lodestars;

(Act I, Scene I)

Yet Helena knows that she is commonly considered to be as beautiful as Hermia. What distresses her is that Demetrius does not share this opinion:

> Through Athens I am thought as fair as she.
> But what of that? Demetrius thinks not so.

(Act I, Scene 1)

If only Demetrius could appreciate her beauty, she believes he would love her, but unfortunately:

> Love looks not with the eyes, but with the mind.

(Act I, Scene 1)

The mind can direct the lover both to see beauty where there is none, and to fail to appreciate real beauty. This, she thinks, has happened to Demetrius.

In Act II, Scene 1, Helena, pursuing Demetrius, sees herself as worthy to be no more than his dog. Later, deserted by Demetrius, she says:

> I am ugly as a bear;
> For beasts that meet me run away for fear.

(Act II, Scene 2)

By now she is so miserable that she has convinced herself that she really is less beautiful than Hermia.

When Lysander wakes and loves her, she speaks of her 'insufficiency' and says she does not even deserve a sweet look from Demetrius. Helena has been depressed by the failure of her eyes to be bright enough to attract Demetrius, so it is significant that when he wakes, he says:

> To what, my love, shall I compare thine eyne?
> Crystal is muddy!

(Act III, Scene 2)

It is not surprising that she regards the behaviour of the men as mockery. However, she is secretly delighted to hear sweet words from Demetrius, and she remembers everything he says:

> Demetrius –
> Who even but now did spurn me with his foot –
> To call me goddess, nymph, divine and rare,
> Precious, celestial?

(Act III, Scene 2)

However, her delight does not prevent her from blaming her own ugliness for the 'jest' and she is unsure enough of herself to think that Hermia is part of the joke. She attacks her for joining with the men to mock her, calling her a 'puppet' and 'lower' than herself thereby much annoying Hermia. However, when she goes to sleep, Helena still believes that the others 'detest' her company. The next morning when Demetrius has not changed his mind again, she seems finally convinced that he loves her, and she worries no more about her beauty.

Clearly, Helena thinks of her beauty in terms of its power to attract Demetrius. While he loves Hermia, she envies Hermia's beauty, even though she knows she is thought to be equally pretty. She easily slips into despondency and convinces herself that she is ugly, until the love of Demetrius restores her confidence.

16. What part is played in *A Midsummer Night's Dream* by Lysander? (O)

Lysander first appears in Act I, Scene 1, when he is presented as Hermia's choice of husband, but is unacceptable to her father, who would prefer Demetrius as a son-in-law. As the matter is placed before the Duke, who must give his judgement, Lysander states his case well:

> My love is more than his;
> My fortunes every way as fairly ranked –
> If not with vantage – as Demetrius',
> And, – which is more than all these boasts can be –
> I am beloved of beauteous Hermia.

(Act I, Scene1)

Later, after lamenting with Hermia the ways in which:

> The course of true love never did run smooth,

(Act I, Scene 1)

he enterprisingly plans an elopement to escape from Athenian law. He and Hermia tell Helena the secret.

In the wood the following night, Lysander and Hermia are lost and tired. They sleep on the turf, after a little good-humoured argument in which Hermia refuses to let Lysander sleep beside her. As he sleeps, Lysander's eyes are anointed by Puck with the result that, when Helena wakes him, and is thus the first person he sees, he falls in love with her and pursues her. He is convinced that 'reason' has persuaded him that she is the 'worthier' maid (Act II, Scene 2).

In Act III, Scene 2, he again tries to convince Helena of the sincerity of his love:

> Look when I vow, I weep; and vows so born,
> In their nativity all truth appears.

When they are joined by Hermia and Demetrius, the inevitable quarrel ensues. Lysander now expresses his hatred for Hermia and declares his love for Helena. When the men decide to duel for Helena's love, Hermia tries to restrain him. He says:

> Hang off, thou cat, thou burr! Vile thing, let loose,
> Or I will shake thee from me like a serpent.

(Act III, Scene 2)

However, he is unwilling to 'hurt' Hermia by using force to get free from her. Like Demetrius, he defends Helena from Hermia when the ladies begin to argue.

Later the men set off to fight, but are prevented from doing so by Puck and Oberon. Lysander's determination does not wane:

> Come, thou gentle day
> For if but once thou show me thy grey light
> I'll find Demetrius and revenge this spite.

(Act III, Scene 2)

While he sleeps, the spell is removed. Consequently, when Theseus wakes him, Lysander loves Hermia once more. He bravely confesses to the Duke and Egeus that he had intended to elope with her.

Theseus uses his power to overrule Egeus and grants Lysander permission to marry Hermia and when the couple next appear, they are husband and wife. This is in Act V, Scene 1, when they watch 'Pyramus and Thisbe', with the other newlyweds, before retiring to bed. Like Theseus and Demetrius, Lysander makes witty comments on the crude presentation. It is he who says of Quince: 'He hath rid his prologue like a rough colt; he knows not the stop.' It is he, too, who caps Demetrius' pun on the word 'die':

BOTTOM *as Pyramus:*
  Now die, die, die, die, die.
DEMETRIUS:
  No die, but an ace for him; for he is but one.
LYSANDER:
  Less than an ace, man; for he is dead. He is nothing.

17. What is the dramatic importance of Act II, Scene 2? (O)

Act II, Scene 2, is the second to be set in the wood near Athens. In the first, we have been introduced to the Fairies, we have heard about the quarrel between Titania and Oberon, and, with Oberon, we have seen Demetrius scorning Helena's love. The stage is set for action to be taken on these matters, and this is what happens in Act II, Scene 2.

Titania sleeps and Oberon squeezes the love juice into her eyes:

> What thou seest when thou dost wake,
> Do it for thy true-love take.

By this action, all is prepared for her brief infatuation with Bottom.

The developments in this scene concerning Demetrius and Helena have more amusing consequences. Puck finds Lysander asleep and wrongly anoints his eyes:

> Who is here?
> Weeds of Athens he doth wear.

The first result of his mistake is apparent in the same scene, for Lysander wakes and sees Helena. He deserts Hermia and follows his new love:

> Hermia, sleep thou there;
> And never mayst thou come Lysander near.

Apart from advancing the stories of Titania and Helena, Act II, Scene 2 has considerable dramatic importance in other ways. It does much to establish the dream-like atmosphere of the middle three acts of the play. It begins with Titania's instructions to the fairies:

> Come, now a roundel and a fairy song
> Then for the third part of a minute hence:
> Some to kill cankers in the muskrose buds,
> Some war with reremice. . . .

This is followed by the lullaby of the fairies and Titania's sleep. Moreover, three other characters become so weary in this scene that they fall asleep. The suggestion of so much sleep, and the fact that the scene is almost entirely in rhyme, give the scene an artificial, dream-like quality.

The scene also has some effective comic moments. There is the good-humoured argument between Hermia and Lysander, in which, though Lysander 'riddles very prettily', Hermia is eventually triumphant. There are the comic effects due to dramatic irony when Puck puts the love juice on Lysander's eyes, and, above all, when Lysander wakes, passionately in love with Helena.

The scene also introduces some new elements into the story. It reveals that Hermia and Lysander fail to reach their intended destination. Lysander admits that he has lost his way. It shows how Demetrius finally escapes from Helena. It also includes Hermia's nightmare, in which, symbolically, Lysander smiles at her suffering.

Act II, Scene 2 has considerable dramatic importance. It develops further the story of Titania and Oberon; complicates the story of the young lovers; creates a dream-like atmosphere; has some very amusing moments; and introduces new elements into the story of *A Midsummer Night's Dream.*

18. What do we learn about the childhood friendship of Helena and Hermia? (O)

In Act III, Scene 2, Helena, suddenly concluding that Hermia has joined the men in a 'confederacy' to mock her, makes a long and passionate speech about the childhood friendship between herself and Hermia. She is furious because her lifelong friend seems to have turned against her, so she reminds Hermia of their long and intimate friendship in order to make her ashamed of her present behaviour. As one would expect, in the heat of her temper, she puts her case strongly, using elaborate and far-fetched similes and other illustrations. The basic argument is that she and Hermia, in their childhood, shared each other's pleasures and secrets and hated to be away from each other.

> Is all the counsel that we two have shared –
> The sisters' vows, the hours that we have spent
> When we have chid the hasty-footed time
> For parting us – O, is all forgot?
> All school-days' friendship, childhood innocence?
> We, Hermia, like two artificial gods
> Have with our needles created both one flower,
> Both on one sampler, sitting on one cushion,
> Both warbling of one song, both in one key,
> As if our hands, our sides, voices, and minds,
> Had been incorporate. So we grew together,
> Like to a double cherry, seeming parted,
> But yet an union in partition.

(Act III, Scene 2)

Earlier in the play, an incident has already illustrated the closeness of their friendship. In Act I, Scene 1, Hermia attempting to console her friend, readily shares her secret with Helena. She telshares her secret with Helena. She tells Helena of the planned elopement, so that Helena may be assured that Demetrius will see Hermia no more. She refers to the place where she and Helena:

> were wont to lie,
> Emptying our bosoms of their counsel sweet

(Act I, Scene 1)

and, on parting, Hermia refers to Helena as:

> sweet playfellow

(Act I, Scene 1)

However, though Shakespeare presents a picture of sincere and enduring friendship, his awareness of the changeability of human nature is too acute to let the matter end there. When the tempers of the women are roused, the less pleasant sides of their characters are revealed. Each believes that the other has deceived her and they exchange insults in bitter fury. Hermia calls Helena a 'canker-blossom' and a 'painted maypole'. Helena calls Hermia a 'counterfeit' and a 'puppet' and, referring again to their childhood intimacy, says:

> She was a vixen when she went to school,
> And though she be but little, she is fierce.

Yet, in the middle of all this rage, Helena can remember:

> I evermore did love you, Hermia;
> Did ever keep your counsels, never wronged you

Clearly, the childhood friendship of Helena and Hermia was very deep and valuable to both. But the realistic characterisation shows that even these two friends' opinions of each other could vary according to circumstances, particularly if, as in this case, it involves competition for the love of a man.

19. What opinions of 'Pyramus and Thisbe' are expressed by (a) Philostrate and (b) Demetrius? (O)

(a) Philostrate believes that 'Pyramus and Thisbe' is unsuitable as entertainment for Duke Theseus and he urges the Duke not to watch it. In his opinion the only pleasure to be derived from the play would be making fun of the craftsmen's feeble efforts:

> it is nothing, nothing in the world;
> Unless you can find sport in their intents,
> Extremely stretched and conned with cruel pain,
> To do you service.

(Act V, Scene 1)

He points out that the actors are amateurs and unskilled in acting:

> Hard-handed men that work in Athens here,
> Which never laboured in their minds till now.

(Act V, Scene 1)

Philostrate formed his opinion of the play when, as Master of the Revels, he saw it rehearsed. He describes it as being some ten words long and, at the same time, ten words too long:

> which makes it 'tedious'. For in all the play
> There is not one word apt, one player fitted.

(Act V, Scene 1)

He explains that, although the play presents the tragedy of Pyramus' death, this scene was so badly acted that it made him laugh.

(b)   Unlike Philostrate, Demetrius does not see the play before its final performance. He is one of those who 'find sport' in commenting on the script and acting.

He has a quick wit and a lively sense of humour. As 'Pyramus and Thisbe' is performed, he becomes increasingly amused by the sport of commenting ironically on the play. His pretended compliments include the following: (of Wall) 'It is the wittiest partition that ever I heard discourse, my lord', and (of Lion) 'The very best at a beast, my lord, that e'er I saw' (Act V, Scene 1). At times his remarks are quite unkind. He says that one lion may talk when 'many asses' do. At times, too, his impertinent comments almost disrupt the performance, as when he criticises Moon for not having horns on his head and for not being inside the lantern.

Principally, however, Demetrius is amused by the play and finds it an admirable foil for his wit. He enjoys being able to toy with ideas it suggests:

LYSANDER   This lion is a very fox for his valour.

THESEUS   True, and a goose for his discretion.

DEMETRIUS Not so, my lord. For his valour cannot carry
                    his discretion; and the fox carries the goose.

(Act V, Scene 1)

20. Summarise the parts played by (a) Hippolyta and (b) any one of Titania's fairies. (O)

(a) Hippolyta appears, with Theseus, in three scenes. In the opening speech of the play, Theseus impatiently looks forward to his marriage to Hippolyta, which is planned to take place four days later. In reply-ing, Hippolyta says:

> Four days will quickly steep themselves in night;
> Four nights will quickly dream away the time.

(Act I, Scene 1)

Comforting Theseus, she also hints at the magical quality of events which are to follow. Hippolyta plays no part in the case which Egeus brings against Hermia and Lysander.

Next, in Act IV, Scene 1, Hippolyta has come to watch the hunt with Theseus. She loves hunting and recalls how she was once with Hercules and Cadmus:

> When in a wood of Crete they bayed the bear.

(Act IV, Scene 1)

She found the cries of the hounds and the echoing sounds delightful:

> I never heard
> So musical a discord, such sweet thunder.

(Act IV, Scene 1)

In Act V, Scene 1, Hippolyta discusses with Theseus the tales told by the young lovers. She is more inclined than Theseus to believe them. Their story is, she says, consistent. It:

> grows to something of great constancy.

(Act V, Scene 1)

When 'Pyramus and Thisbe' is proposed as entertainment, Hippolyta says:

> I love not to see wretchedness o'ercharged,
> And duty in his service perishing.

(Act V, Scene 1)

But Theseus insists on watching the play. At times, Hippolyta seems a little irritated by the performance. However, she joins in with the comments made by the men, and, incidentally, is the only one of the women to do so.

(b) The fairy 'Cobweb' first appears in Act II, Scene 1, where he is one of four fairies in attendance on Titania during the quarrel with Oberon.

In the following scene, with the other fairies, he receives orders from Titania and sings the lullaby which helps the Fairy Queen to sleep. He leaves Titania before Oberon arrives.

In Act III, Scene 1, he is recalled by Titania, who is now awake and in love with Bottom. With the others, he is told what service to give to Bottom, who says to him: 'if I cut my finger, I shall make bold with you.' (Since it was believed in Shakespeare's time that cobwebs put on a cut could help stop the bleeding). Cobweb and the other fairies attend to Bottom's needs in Act IV, Scene 1. Bottom orders Cobweb to: 'kill me a red-hipped humble-bee on the top of a thistle, and, good Monsieur, bring me the honey bag' (Act IV, Scene 1). Cobweb must be careful not to 'fret' himself and must not let the honey bag burst all over him. Cobweb helps the others to scratch Bottom's head and is then sent away on his duties by Titania.

Finally, Cobweb takes part in the song and dance, near the end of the play. This appropriately precedes the final two speeches of the play, Oberon's benediction and Puck's epilogue.

21. 'The characters of Demetrius and Lysander are very similar.' Show how far you consider this statement true. (O)

At the beginning of the play, Demetrius has a reputation for being unfaithful. He:

> Made love to Nedar's daughter, Helena,
> And won her soul

(Act I, Scene 1)

Now, however, he loves Hermia. Lysander on the other hand, seems to love Hermia devotedly, although he is as cruel to her when he is under the influence of the love juice as Demetrius is to Helena.

Both Demetrius and Lysander are commonly regarded as 'worthy gentlemen'. Even Theseus in Act I, Scene 1, acknowledges this fact. Both men make devoted, passionate speeches to the women they love and yet are capable of speaking in a cruel and harsh way to the women of whom they wish to rid themselves. Examples are:

LYSANDER (To Helena)

> Look when I vow, I weep; and vows so born,
> In their nativity all truth appears.

(Act III, Scene 2)

LYSANDER (To Hermia)

> Thy love? out, tawny Tartar, out;
> Out, loathèd medicine! O hated potion, hence!

(Act III, Scene 2)

DEMETRIUS (to Helena)

> Tempt not too much the hatred of my spirit;
> For I am sick when I do look on thee.

(Act II, Scene 1)

DEMETRIUS (to Helena)

> To what, my love, shall I compare thine eyne?
> Crystal is muddy! O, how ripe in show
> Thy lips – those kissing cherries – tempting grow!

(Act III, Scene 2)

Clearly both men have strong passions and emotions and, similarly, when they are roused, both are very brave. At the end of Act III, each is prepared to risk his own life in a duel in order to prove his love for Helena.

In cooler moments both men have a good sense of humour and a ready wit. When watching 'Pyramus and Thisbe', they join with Theseus in making jokes suggested to them by the play and by each other's wit:

PYRAMUS   Now die, die, die, die, die.

DEMETRIUS No die, but an ace for him, for he is but one.

LYSANDER Less than an ace, man; for he is dead. He is nothing.

(Act V, Scene 1)

The characters of Demetrius and Lysander are clearly very similar. Although it is possible to regard Lysander as a more unwavering lover than Demetrius, in all other respects, their characters are alike. Both are gentlemen, capable of strong passions; both are brave and have a good sense of humour.

22. Give an account, in the right order, of the work done by Puck. (O)

Puck first appears in Act II, Scene 1, when we learn from his conversation with the Fairy that he enjoys, and frequently plays, mischievous pranks such as imitating a 'threefoot stool' and then slipping from under the 'wisest aunt' as she sits on him. He also brings good luck to those who call him 'Hobgoblin' or 'Sweet Puck'.

The first constructive work he is given to do in the play occurs when he is sent by Oberon to fetch the flower called 'love in idleness', which contains the magic love juice. Setting off, Puck says:

> I'll put a girdle round about the earth
> In forty minutes!

(Act II, Scene 1)

While he is absent, Oberon overhears the conversation during which Demetrius continues to reject Helena. When Puck returns, Oberon gives him the task of anointing the eyes of Demetrius so that he will fall in love with Helena.

In the following scene Puck does his best to carry out Oberon's instruction. He finds a man wearing:

> 'weeds of Athens'

(Act II, Scene 2)

with a lady asleep some distance away. Concluding that Lysander is, in fact, Demetrius, he applies the love juice:

> Churl, upon thy eyes I throw
> All the power this charm doth owe.

(Act II, Scene 2)

It is Oberon, and not Puck, who undertakes the task of anointing Titania's eyes, but it is Puck's work which leads to her falling in love with an ass. During the rehearsal by the craftsmen Puck places the ass's head on Bottom and continues to torment and terrify Bottom's friends:

> I'll follow you, I'll lead you about a round,
> Thorough bog, thorough bush, thorough brake, thorough briar

(Act III, Scene 1)

With delight he relates to Oberon what has happened (Act III, Scene 2). Returning to the problem of the young lovers, Oberon orders Puck to draw Helena to that spot where Oberon himself anoints the eyes of Demetrius. Puck goes:

> Swifter than arrow from the Tartar's bow.

(Act III, Scene 2)

and returns almost at once, with both Helena and Lysander. Later in this same scene Puck is given the work of preventing Lysander and Demetrius from coming to blows. Gleefully he obeys Oberon's instructions, first by producing a fog and then by imitating the voices of Demetrius and Lysander alternately:

> Follow my voice. We'll try no manhood here.
>
> (Act III, Scene 2)

When all four lovers are assembled and asleep, Puck, again on Oberon's instructions, performs the very important task of applying a second juice to the eyes of Lysander. It is this juice which cancels the effects of the first:

> When thou wakest,
> Thou takest
> True delight
> In the sight
> Of thy former lady's eye.
>
> (Act III, Scene 2)

In Act IV, Scene 1, Puck is ordered to remove Bottom's ass' head. He does so promptly, saying:

> Now when thou wakest with thine own fool's eyes peep.
>
> (Act IV, Scene 1)

At the end of the play Puck has two final tasks. First, in Duke Theseus' court, he helps with household chores:

> I am sent with broom before
> To sweep the dust behind the door.
>
> (Act V, Scene 1)

Second, in the play's epilogue, he leaves the actors on good terms with the audience and weaves the dream into the reality of the audience:

> If we shadows have offended,
> Think but this, and all is mended:
> That you have but slumbered here
> While these visions did appear.
> And this weak and idle theme,
> No more yielding but a dream,
> Gentles, do not reprehend.
> If you pardon, we will mend.
>
> (Act V, Scene 1)

23. Are the fairies invisible to all of the mortals? What does their invisibility add to the fun of the play? (O)

The only mortal to whom the fairies are not invisible is Bottom. He is able to see Titania and her attendants. This, in itself, is a source of amusement, since, particularly when he has his ass' head, Bottom is a gross and most un-fairylike mortal. The contrast between him and Titania and the incongruity of the scene in which she 'winds' him in her arms are amusing.

The invisibility of the fairies to all other mortals adds greatly to the fun. This is particularly true of the antics of Puck and Oberon. First, in

Act II, Scene 1, Oberon is able to listen, unseen, to the quarrel between Demetrius and Helena:

> I am invisible,
> And I will overhear their conference.

(Act II, Scene 1)

One can imagine the actor playing the part of Oberon extracting a good deal of amusement from this scene by means of facial expressions, as he reacts to the harsh words of Demetrius. Equally important, however, is the fact that Oberon's invisibility enables him to become acquainted with Helena's plight. His decision to help her leads directly to all the amusing confusion later on. Puck accidentally anoints the wrong man and Oberon, to put things right, anoints the right one with the result that, for a time, both men love Helena.

Meanwhile Puck's invisibility contributes to the fun of Act II, Scene 1:

> What, a play toward? I'll be an auditor –
> An actor too, perhaps, if I see cause.

(Act III, Scene 1)

He does see cause and places the ass' head on Bottom. This ruins the rehearsal, terrifies the other craftsmen and leads to Titania's being awakened by, and falling in love with, Bottom.

During the whole of the lovers' quarrel (Act III, Scene 2) Oberon and Puck are present but invisible. Here again good actors would find ample opportunity for making the audience laugh by their reactions to the hot-tempered words of the four young people. By the end of the scene Puck's invisibility causes still more comedy and confusion. Though he is invisible, he is not inaudible, and he misleads and torments Demetrius and Lysander by imitating the voices of each of them in turn.

Clearly a great deal of the comedy in Acts II and III is due to the invisibility of the fairies. When they are on the stage at the same time as the mortals, their reactions to the mortals' words are a source of fun. In addition, their interference in human affairs complicates the plot and provides some amusing moments.

24. What is the dramatic importance of the closing moments of *A Midsummer Night's Dream* – after the Athenian craftsmen have finished their play? (O)

The closing moments of *A Midsummer Night's Dream* are dramatically important in several ways.

In these lines the various tales told in the play are finally brought to their happy conclusions. The Athenian craftsmen have performed 'Pyramus and Thisbe' to their own satisfaction and round things off very well with Theseus' permission by dancing a Bergomask (rustic dance). The Duke thanks and congratulates the actors for their performance which was 'notably discharged'. He is no longer impatiently awaiting his 'nuptial hour', and the young lovers, too, with their problems sorted out, are married. All the newlyweds retire to bed. Theseus announces that there will be celebrations for the next fortnight. Even the story of Titania and Oberon is now brought to a happy conclusion, for they are reunited and dance together. All these details create an atmosphere of happiness and satisfaction.

The closing moments of the play are also important for the way in which they blend the worlds of fantasy and reality, giving the impression that the fairy kingdom is at hand, invisible but benevolent, ensuring the continued happiness of the mortals. Puck's speech creates the right atmosphere:

> Now it is the time of night
> That the graves, all gaping wide,
> Every one lets forth his sprite
> In the churchway paths to glide.

> (Act V, Scene 1)

He himself has come to help with household chores.

The visual effect of the fairies' dance and the use of rhyme by Puck, Oberon and Titania all have dramatic importance, since they create an atmosphere of magic and the supernatural, in which spells may be successfully cast. When the impression has been established, Oberon prepares to cast his spell. He will go to the best bride bed:

> Which by us shall blessèd be;
> And the issue there create
> Ever shall be fortunate.

> (Act V, Scene 1)

This carries the feeling of happiness and well-being into the future too, and is therefore an important contribution to the joyful ending of *A Midsummer Night's Dream*.

Yet one more speech remains, the epilogue spoken by Puck. This also has dramatic importance for three reasons. Firstly, it helps to awaken the audience from the world of fantasies and dreams and to restore them to the real world outside the theatre. Secondly, it offers an apology to those who have found the play's theme trivial:

> If we shadows have offended,
> Think but this and all is mended,
> That you have but slumbered here
> While these visions did appear,
> And this weak and idle theme,
> No more yielding but a dream.

> (Act V, Scene 1)

68

Thirdly, it leaves the actors on good terms with the audience, and makes a promise to make amends in the near future if the play has offended:

> If we have unearned luck
> Now to scape the serpent's tongue
> We will make amends ere long,
> Else the Puck a liar call.
> So, good night unto you all.
> Give me your hands if we be friends
> And Robin shall restore amends.

MODEL ANSWERS
A LEVEL STANDARD

CONTENTS Page

34. Theseus says: 'Never any thing can be amiss,
                    When simpleness and duty tender it'.
Do you find the qualities of simpleness and duty in the
character of Peter Quince? What other qualities has he?   **85**

35. Comment on Shakespeare's use of rhyme in *A Midsummer
Night's Dream*.   **87**

36. At what times do you feel pity for (a) Hermia, and (b)
Helena? Explain how this pity is evoked.   **88**

37. 'Theseus appears in only three scenes and yet his role
is very important.' Discuss.   **90**

38. 'In *A Midsummer Night's Dream*, several characters
sleep on the stage and their sleep serves to actuate
the plot.' Discuss and illustrate this statement.   **92**

25. By quoting four examples, show how Shakespeare uses figurative expressions to describe changes in characters' attitudes to one another. (A)

(i) HELENA:

> He hailed down oaths that he was only mine,
> And when this hail some heat from Hermia felt,
> So he dissolved, and showers of oaths did melt.

Here Helena is speaking of the way in which Demetrius ceased to love her and loved Hermia instead. Her metaphor is based on the idea of hail dissolving in heat. Once Demetrius 'hailed' vows of love on Helena. The hail was then affected by heat from Hermia and his love for Helena, like the hail, melted.

(ii) LYSANDER:

> Things growing are not ripe until their season.
> So I, being young, till now ripe not to reason.
> And touching now the point of human skill,
> Reason becomes the marshall to my will,
> And leads me to your eyes . . . .

Lysander awakes from his sleep to find that he now loves Helena, and not Hermia. He tries to explain the new attitude by a metaphor about growing things, such as plants. Just as they take time to reach maturity, to become 'ripe', so his reason has taken time to mature. Now, his reason is mature, and directs him to his new love.

(iii) DEMETRIUS:

> My heart to her but as guestwise sojourned,
> And now to Helen is it home returned,
> There to remain.

Demetrius originally loved Helena. Then, for a time, he loved Hermia. Now he loves Helena again. Here he explains his new attitude to Hermia, whom he wishes to leave to Lysander, without further competition. His feeble explanation takes the form of a simile in which he implies that his heart has always been at 'home' with Helena but spent some time as a guest of Hermia.

(iv) DEMETRIUS:

>   my love to Hermia,
> Melted as the snow, seems to me now
> As the remembrance of an idle gaud
> Which in my childhood I did dote upon;
> And all the faith, the virtue of my heart,
> The object and the pleasure of mine eye,

> Is only Helena. To her, my lord,
> Was I betrothed ere I saw Hermia;
> But like in sickness did I loathe this food.
> But, as in health come to my natural taste,
> Now I do wish it, love it . . . .

In front of Duke Theseus, Demetrius has to make a further attempt to explain how his love returned to Helena. He uses a number of similes to do this. His love for Hermia 'melted' as the snow. It now seems like a plaything he once had as a child. His final analogy likens his love for Helena with a sick man's desire for food. During his sickness he had no desire for the food of Helena's love. Now he considers himself to be well again.

26. 'The course of true love never did run smooth.' In what ways does *A Midsummer Night's Dream* illustrate this statement? (A)

It is Lysander who observes, in Act I, Scene 1, that:
> The course of true love never did run smooth

and he and Hermia lament the several ways in which true love's course may be impeded.

Difficulties, they say, may be due to differences in social status between the lovers, or to differences in their ages, or to the fact that marriage partners are chosen by others. Moreover, even when the lovers gladly accepted the choice:

> War, death, or sickness did lay siege to it,
> Making it momentany as a sound,
> Swift as a shadow, short as any dream.

(Act I, Scene 1)

So from an early point in the play, Lysander and Hermia indicate this central theme of *A Midsummer Night's Dream*. Their own experiences are a further illustration of the difficulties of true love. First, they are opposed by Hermia's father, who wants her to marry Demetrius. Next, when they flee, they lose their way in the wood, with the result that they fail to get beyond the bounds of Athenian law which threatens to execute Hermia if she refuses to marry Demetrius, and also fall victim to the misapplied magic of Oberon and Puck. Hermia remains faithful to Lysander and fights for her love even when Lysander claims he loves Helena. Finally, when the sleeping lovers are found by Theseus, it seems for a moment that they will have to be punished by Athenian law after all, until the Duke overrules Egeus.

For Helena and Demetrius, too, there is no smooth course for true love. Like Hermia, Helena remains faithful to the man she loves, even when jilted by him. She pursues the: 'hard-hearted adamant' to the wood and is the victim of misery and misapprehension before, by the kindness of Oberon, Demetrius' love for her is restored, and she finally becomes convinced that he loves her.

However, it is not only the experiences of the four young lovers which illustrate the difficulties of true love. Even the Fairy King and Queen have their quarrel. Oberon is annoyed with his wife because she will not give him the changeling boy. Also, each is jealous of the other's love for mortals. As a result of the quarrel, Titania tells her fairies:

> I have forsworn his bed and company
>
> (Act II, Scene 1)

The situation persists for some time, while Oberon torments Titania by causing her to fall in love with Bottom, and obtains the changeling boy from her.

Finally, he says:

> Her dotage now I do begin to pity
>
> (Act IV, Scene 1)

and he releases her from the magic charm. The Fairy King and Queen are happily reunited.

In other ways, too, the play illustrates the difficulties of true love. The love of Theseus for Hippolyta seems true enough, but as we learn from Oberon, Theseus had loved four women before. Oberon says to Titania:

> Didst thou not lead him through the glimmering night
> From Perigenia, whom he ravishèd,
> And make him with fair Aegles break his faith,
> With Ariadne, and Antiopa?
>
> (Act II, Scene 1)

Even 'Pyramus and Thisbe', though very comical in its performance by the craftsmen, illustrates how true love can have a sad outcome. Pyramus and Thisbe are obliged to meet secretly, away from their families. As a result of a misunderstanding, both commit suicide. A tomb must cover even the beautiful eyes, 'green as leeks', of Pyramus. All the other lovers, having now overcome their own misfortunes, can laugh at this fiction played out before them.

27.   **˙'Thou shalt know the man**
      By the Athenian garments he hath on.'
Show why this quotation from Act II, Scene 1, is of considerable importance to later events in the play.   **(A)**

Following the quarrel between Oberon and Titania, early in Act II, Scene 1, Oberon sends Puck away to fetch the flower 'love-in-idleness', which he intends to squeeze on the eyes of Titania. The heated conversation between Demetrius and Helena occurs after Puck's departure, so that it is Oberon alone who hears it.

This point is very important to one of the plots interwoven in *A Midsummer Night's Dream.* If Puck had heard the harsh words of Demetrius, he would have known who Demetrius was. However by the time Puck returns with the potion Demetrius and Helena have gone. Oberon decides that, as well as tormenting Titania, he will use the magic powers of the juice to help Helena by having it applied to Demetrius' eyes. He tells his plan to Puck:

> A sweet Athenian lady is in love
> With a disdainful youth – anoint his eyes. . . .

(Act II, Scene 1)

As Puck does not know Demetrius, Oberon has to describe him, and he does so perfunctorily:

> Thou shalt know the man
> By the Athenian garments he hath on.

(Act II, Scene 1)

Consequently when Puck comes upon the sleeping Lysander, he reasonably supposes him to be the man in question:

> Weeds of Athens he doth wear.
> This is he my master said
> Despisèd the Athenian maid;
> And here the maiden, sleeping sound
> On the dank and dirty ground.
> Pretty soul she durst not lie
> Near this lack-love, this kill-courtesy.

(Act II, Scene 2)

Puck applies the juice; a few moments later Lysander is awakened by Helena and he immediately falls in love with her. Thus, as a result of a careless description by Oberon, a series of events is triggered off, which is confusing to the lovers and very amusing to the audience. Puck, too, enjoys the joke:

> Lord, what fools these mortals be!

(Act III, Scene 2)

Meanwhile, Oberon and Puck, seeing how Hermia speaks to Demetrius, have discovered their mistake. Oberon says:

> What hast thou done? Thou hast mistaken quite,
> And laid the love juice on some true love's sight.

(Act III, Scene 2)

The Fairy King plans at once to rectify the mistake by anointing the eyes of Demetrius and drawing Helena to the spot where he sleeps. However, Lysander still loves Helena, so there follows the amusing scene in which two men love one woman and decide to fight a duel. The women, too, quarrel and come near to blows. It is not until all four lovers are asleep that Oberon can finish correcting his mistake.

Clearly the description of Demetrius given by Oberon to Puck has considerable importance. It leads to great confusion for the lovers and provides some of the play's most lively comedy. Eventually Oberon rectifies the mistake and much more good than harm is done in so far as all four are accommodated whereas without intervention Demetrius would not have changed his mind about Helena.

28. Egeus' objections to Lysander and his preference for Demetrius as a husband for his daughter are based not on logical reasoning but on blind prejudice.' Discuss this opinion. (A)

It is true that, if we examine Egeus' objections to Lysander and his preference for Demetrius, we shall find no logical reasoning behind them. In the first place, he does not take his daughter's wishes into account. Hermia's choice is quite decidedly Lysander. Secondly, he does not consider Demetrius' reputation. It is well known that Demetrius had first wooed and won Helena before switching his affections to Hermia. This does not suggest great stability of character and hardly renders him an ideal prospective son-in-law. Moreover, as Duke Theseus himself agrees, Lysander is just as 'worthy' a gentleman as Demetrius. Egeus gives no reason at all for his preference for Demetrius. He only says:

> This man hath my consent to marry her.
>
> (Act I, Scene 1)

When he speaks of Lysander, he gives what seems to him to be logical reasons for objecting to this man, though it would be hard for anyone else to see them in that light. He accuses Lysander of bewitching his daughter and says to him:

> Thou, thou, Lysander, thou hast given her rhymes,
> And interchanged love-tokens with my child.
> Thou hast by moonlight at her window sung
> With feigning voice verses of feigning love,
> And stolen the impression of her fantasy.
> With bracelets of thy hair, rings, gauds, conceits,
> Knacks, trifles, nosegays, sweetmeats – messengers
> Of strong prevailment in unhardened youth –
> With cunning hast thou filched my daughter's heart,
> Turned her obedience which is due to me
> To stubborn harshness.
>
> (Act I, Scene 1)

From Lysander's behaviour we deduce that his love for Hermia and her love for him are certainly real, so it seems unreasonable that Egeus should use such words as 'feigning' and 'cunning' of Lysander and 'unhardened' of Hermia. Lysander's courtship of Hermia, though his language may sound strange and elaborate today, is surely reasonable.

Egeus' objections to the presents given to Hermia are based entirely on prejudice. His view of the courtship is too subjective to be based on logical reasoning. His final remarks suggest that he is a cruel parent, demanding obedience to his will even in this matter, and possibly there is fear and jealousy in his attitude to Lysander, since this is the man who wants to take Hermia away and who has caused her to disobey her father.

When the lovers are discovered in the wood (Act IV, Scene 1), Egeus' attitude is unchanged. Still he fails to acknowledge that Lysander's love for Hermia is sincere. On the contrary, he instantly demands: 'the law, the law upon his head'. Blind prejudice leads him to see only one side of the matter, namely that Lysander and Hermia, by eloping, have sought to cheat him and Demetrius.

Clearly Egeus is not reasonable in his opposition to Lysander. Since Hermia loves Lysander and he loves her, and Demetrius has jilted her, reason would approve Lysander. However, unmitigated prejudice seems to guide Egeus, for he chooses to believe that Lysander is deceiving Hermia, and has a selfish desire to impose his own will on her.

29.   'Then will two at once woo one –
         That must needs be sport alone'

                                        (Act III, Scene 2)

Describe the 'sport' which follows this prediction by Puck.   (A)

Puck, with delighted expectation, looks forward to the 'sport' which will ensue when Lysander and Helena enter the part of the wood where Demetrius is asleep, his eyes anointed with the love juice. Lysander already loves Helena and is making his protestations to her:

> Look when I vow, I weep

                                        (Act III, Scene 2)

As Puck expects, Demetrius awakes and instantly addresses Helena with words of love:

> O Helen, goddess, nymph, perfect, divine –
> To what, my love, shall I compare thine eyne?
> Crystal is muddy! . . . .

                                        (Act III, Scene 2)

Helena, knowing that both men loved Hermia only a short while before, is convinced that they are making fun of her:

> You both are rivals, and love Hermia;
> And now both rivals, to mock Helena.
> A trim exploit, a manly enterprise –
> To conjure tears up in a poor maid's eyes
> With your derision.

(Act III, Scene 2)

Each of the men, too, thinks that the other is mocking Helena and each offers to the other his claim to Hermia's love.

Hermia herself arrives at this moment and is happy to find Lysander again. When he tells her that he hates her now, she can reply only in amazement:

> You speak not as you think: It cannot be.

(Act III, Scene 2)

Helena's reaction to this adds to the 'sport'. She believes Hermia has joined the men in a 'confederacy' to mock her. She reminds Hermia of their happy childhood together and is amazed that her friend should now insult her in this way. Dramatic irony makes the 'sport' all the more enjoyable since Puck and the audience know that Hermia is entirely innocent. Though Hermia repeatedly declares that she does not understand what is happening, Helena accuses her of 'setting on' the men.

When Helena again scorns the 'jest' and tries to leave, the men resume their declarations of sincerity. Their thoughts soon turn to a duel, since each wishes to prove his love with his own life. Hermia seizes Lysander, and Demetrius scorns him for being held by such a 'weak bond'. Lysander, trying to free himself from Hermia's grasp, abuses her in strong terms and says to Demetrius:

> What? Should I hurt her, strike her, kill her dead?
> Although I hate her, I'll not harm her so.

(Act III, Scene 2)

At last he convinces Hermia that he really loves Helena, and the 'sport' is wryly humorous as we watch Hermia's reaction, instead of blaming Lysander for his unfaithfulness she blames Helena for stealing his heart. The comedy here is due both to dramatic irony and to Shakespeare's mockery of the jealous rivalry of the two women.

30.   *A tedious brief scene of young Pyramus*
               And his love Thisbe; 'very tragical mirth'.

How well does the final presentation of 'Pyramus and Thisbe' live up to this description of it in the 'brief'?   **(A)**

Theseus is amazed that a play can be:

> Merry and tragical? Tedious and brief?

> (Act V, Scene 1)

Yet, the presentation of 'Pyramus and Thisbe' does live up to this contradictory description.

It is tedious in the sense that, as Philostrate says, it is some ten words long:

> But by ten words, my lord, it is too long,
> Which makes it 'tedious'. For in all the play
> There is not one word apt, one player fitted.

> (Act V, Scene 1)

It is tedious, too, because unimportant details in the story are dwelt on at length while more important matters are skipped over. There is a long prologue by Quince, which tells at length the story with which Theseus and his friends are already well acquainted. There are the unnecessary speeches by Wall, Lion and Moonshine and the long addresses of Pyramus to the Night and to the Moon. There are the melodramatic suicide speeches, full of pathos, spoken by Pyramus and Thisbe. Moreover, most of these tedious speeches contain rhetorical effects used for their own sake. One is apostrophe:

> O grim-looked night, O night with hue so black

and another is alliteration:

> He bravely broached his boiling bloody breast.

These would please the actors but could well seem tedious to the audience.

The play is 'brief' because, apart from the tedious speeches, there is practically nothing else in it.

It is 'tragical' in the sense that its story is a sad tale of two young people whose loves, like those of Hero and Leander or Romeo and Juliet, lead to their own deaths.

Finally, the play is full of 'mirth' in many senses. In any theatrical presentation of *A Midsummer Night's Dream,* the actors find many ways of adding to the fun implicit in the words Shakespeare has given them to speak. Thisbe's voice, Pyramus' overacting, the nervousness of Moonshine, the ways in which the actors move, can all be sources of amusement. A good deal of 'mirth' is also to be found in the words Shakespeare has written. Quince's misuse of punctuation has amusing effects:

> All for your delight
> We are not here.

The versification of the script is so feeble as to be laughable:

> The trusty Thisbe coming first by night
> Did scare away, or rather did affright.

and

> O night which ever art when day is not!
> O night, O night, alack, alack, alack

Bottom's behaviour in speaking directly to the audience is amusing because it is so incongruous. Also, there are the many inappropriate words and phrases. Examples of these are:

> Sweet Moon, I thank thee for thy sunny beams

and

> His eyes were green as leeks.

Paradoxical though they are, the promises of being 'tedious brief' and 'tragical mirth' are fulfilled by 'Pyramus and Thisbe'.

31. Helena says of Hermia: 'though she be but little, she is fierce'. What evidence is there to support Helena's opinion and what other characteristics do you observe in Hermia? (A)

There is evidence to support Helena's opinion that Hermia is little, but fierce. It is to be found in Act III, Scene 2, when Hermia, believing that Helena has stolen Lysander's love, returns insult for insult with Helena. Having been scorned as a 'counterfeit' and a 'puppet', she derides Helena's superior height and even threatens to claw at her eyes:

> How low am I, thou painted maypole? Speak!
> How low am I? – I am not yet so low
> But that my nails can reach into thine eyes.

> (Act III, Scene 2)

However, the point must be made that this streak of fierceness is apparent only when she is under great provocation. In addition, her words are clearly spoken in the heat of temper. Of her other characteristics, that which comes closest to fierceness in her character is stubbornness. She has the courage of her convictions and is steadfast in her affections. She stands up bravely to her father and to Duke Theseus in Act I, Scene 1, when both men urge her to accept Demetrius:

> So will I grow, so live, so die, my Lord,
> Ere I will yield my virgin patent up
> Unto his lordship, whose unwishèd yoke
> My soul consents not to give sovereignty.

> (Act I, Scene 1)

preferring to verbalise her opinions than submit quietly.

Other characteristics of Hermia are the loyalty and devotion in her love for Lysander. She is prepared to die for him; she elopes with him; she remains faithful even when he deserts her, and she accuses Helena rather than Lysander of being responsible for this defection. When he sets off to prove with his life his love for Helena, Hermia can still say:

> Heavens shield Lysander, if they mean a fray.

(Act III, Scene 2)

The story of her love for Lysander reveals another characteristic, namely her bold and resourceful manner of coping with problems. When he suggests leaving Athens, she consents without hesitation:

> By all the vows that ever men have broke –
> In number more than ever women spoke, –
> In that same place thou hast appointed me
> Tomorrow truly will I meet with thee.

(Act I, Scene I)

She also has the integrity to do only what she believes – although willing to elope with Lysander she determindly dissuades him from sleeping beside her in the wood,

> But, gentle friend, for love and courtesy
> Lie further off, in human modesty:
> Such separation as may well be said
> Becomes a virtuous bachelor and a maid,
> So far be distant, and good night, sweet friend;
> Thy love ne'er alter till thy sweet life end.

(Act II, Scene 2)

Finally, one observes in Hermia the qualities of kindness and generosity. She comforts Helena by giving away the secret of the planned elopement:

> Take comfort. He no more shall see my face.
> Lysander and myself will fly this place.

(Act I, Scene 1)

Later she is kind to Helena for as long as her patience permits. She says to Lysander: 'Sweet, do not scorn her so.' (Act III, Scene 2).

To conclude, Hermia is fierce, but only when greatly provoked. She is stubborn when convinced that she is in the right. As a lover, she is loyal and devoted, even in the face of infidelity. She is enterprising, kind and generous.

32. 'In the commingling of fantasy and reality, the use of the word "dream" is itself of considerable importance.' On what occasions and with what effects is the word 'dream' used? **(A)**

The word 'dream' is first used in the opening exchange of the play when Hippolyta says to Theseus:

> Four nights will quickly dream away the time
>
> (Act I, Scene 1)

The time she is referring to is that which has yet to pass before her wedding to Theseus. The effect of the word is to prepare us for the dreamy atmosphere which will prevail during that time, while supernatural and confused events take place.

Next, Lysander says to Hermia that love, if destroyed by war, death or sickness, proves; 'short as any dream' (Act I, Scene 1). This makes us think that love can be transitory, and this proves to be a theme in later events, as in Lysander's love for Helena, or Titania's for Bottom.

The third use of 'dream' refers to the occasion when Hermia wakes from a dream in which she saw Lysander, sitting by, smiling, while a serpent ate away at her heart. 'Dream' serves particularly well here to mingle fantasy with reality, for her dream symbolises what has really happened: when she went to sleep, Lysander loved her; now he hates her.

After the dream-like incidents of Acts II and III, various characters, looking back on past events, use the word 'dream' in attempting to describe them. Oberon, in Act IV, Scene 1, says that Bottom will think of the night's events 'as the fierce vexation of a dream'. Sure enough, Bottom, waking a few moments later, says: 'I have had a dream, past the wit of man to say what dream it was . . .'
He returns to his friends and the world of reality, and the word 'dream' has been an important link between the two.

Similarly, when Demetrius, wakes he regards the recent past as a dream:

> These things seem small and undistinguishable,
> Like far-off mountains turnèd into clouds.
>
> (Act IV, Scene 1)

He says later:

> Are you sure
> That we are awake? It seems to me
> That yet we sleep, we dream.
>
> (Act IV, Scene 1)

The effect of waking from a dream before returning to reality is completed by Puck in the last speech of the play, when he says to the audience:

> Think but this, and all is mended:
> That you have but slumbered here
> While these visions did appear.
> And this weak and idle theme,
> No more yielding but a dream.

(Act V, Scene 1)

The word 'dream' is important in the mingling of fantasy with reality. It is first used to make us expect events as confused as those in dreams, and, later, when various characters look back on the events we are guided back into the world of reality.

33. 'The beautiful word-pictures in the speeches of Oberon serve greatly to create the illusion of a dream.' With reference to examples from Oberon's speeches show why you agree or disagree with this opinion. (A)

To create the illusion of a dream on stage using human actors is extremely difficult. The 19th Century critic Hazlitt pointed out that human beings playing the parts of fairies are incredible. He thought *A Midsummer Night's Dream* could succeed only in print: 'The boards of a theatre and the regions of fancy are not the same thing.'

Probably, most people experience the same difficulty as Hazlitt when watching the play and Shakespeare must have anticipated this reaction. Far from trying to sustain the illusion, Shakespeare forces the discrepancies on the audience so that they can only overcome the problem by a definite exertion of imagination.

Oberon, however, is the particular character who does most to create the illusion of unreality. Although a fairy, he is described in human terms so that only a limited suspension of disbelief is asked for from the audience. More importantly his speeches have the effect of hypnosis; we are held under the spell of the world he creates in his words.

In Act II, Scene 1, he relates to Puck how Cupid's arrow once fell upon the flower 'love-in-idleness.' First, he says:

> Thou rememberest
> Since once I sat upon a promontory
> And heard a mermaid on a dolphin's back
> Uttering such dulcet and harmonious breath
> That the rude sea grew civil at her song,
> And certain stars shot madly from their spheres
> To hear the sea maid's music?

(Act II, Scene 1)

The fanciful ideas, especially the behaviour of the sea and stars, the beautiful cadences and the perfect choice of words all serve to create the necessary dream-like picture in the minds of the listeners. Cupid's arrow was:

> Quenched in the chaste beams of the watery moon.

This lovely line appeals at once to our senses and our sensitivity and lulls us into accepting the illusion of a dream.

In the same scene Oberon describes the place where Titania sleeps. His fanciful, luscious and pictorial description again works on our minds to achieve far more than the physical appearance of Titania and any amount of fine scenery on the stage:

> I know a bank where the wild thyme blows,
> Where oxlips and the nodding violet grows,
> Quite overcanopied with luscious woodbine,
> With sweet muskroses and with eglantine.
> There sleeps Titania some time of the night,
> Lulled in these flowers with dances and delight.
> And there the snake throws her enamelled skin,
> Weed wide enough to wrap a fairy in.

A further example of an occasion when Oberon's words feed our imagination occurs in Act IV, Scene 1. Describing a subject gross in itself – the adornment of Bottom by Titania – he gives it a dream-like quality through his exquisite and enchanting choice of words and ideas:

> For she his hairy temples then had rounded
> With coronet of fresh and fragrant flowers.
> And that same dew, which sometime on the buds
> Was wont to swell, like round and orient pearls,
> Stood now within the pretty flowerets' eyes
> Like tears that did their own disgrace bewail.

> (Act IV, Scene 1)

As these examples have shown, Oberon's 'beautiful word-pictures' serve greatly to create the illusion of a dream.

34. Theseus says:

> 'never any thing can be amiss,
> When simpleness and duty tender it.'

Do you find the qualities of simpleness and duty in the character of Peter Quince? What other qualities has he? (A)

Peter Quince, the carpenter, who is stage manager of 'Pyramus and Thisbe' certainly has the qualities of simpleness and duty. He proudly presents, in Act I, Scene 2 'the scroll of every man's name which is thought fit through all Athens to play in our interlude before the Duke and Duchess on his wedding day at night.' His simpleness and duty are

obvious here, and later, too, when he naïvely consents to the suggestions of the others that prologues should be written to inform the ladies
that no one is really being killed and that the Lion is only Snug the
Joiner. It does not occur to him that courtiers would be quite familiar
not only with the illusions of drama but also with the story of Pyramus
and Thisbe.

His simplicity is evident in many other places. He misuses words
without any awareness of the incongruous results, for example: Bottom is a 'very paramour for a sweet voice' (Act IV, Scene 2) and the
Prologue to the play is read without paying heed to punctuation marks:

> We do not come as minding to content you,
> Our true intent is. All for your delight
> We are not here . . . .

(Act V, Scene 1)

Within the limits of his endearing qualities of simpleness and duty,
Quince has other qualities. First, he is easy-going. He readily accepts
the opinions of the others and consents to their suggestions for prologues, though this means more work for himself. Unlike Bottom he
has no desire to be the star performer but is content, in the original
plan, to play the part of Thisbe's father.

He is as shrewd and thoughtful as his simplicity allows. It is he who
recommends rehearsing away from public view and it is he who raises
the problems of producing moonlight and a wall. When the craftsmen
first arrive in the wood, it is he who observes how well the spot suits the
requirements of a drama company: 'This green plot shall be our stage,
this hawthorn-brake our tiring-house' (Act III, Scene 1). He also sets
about directing the rehearsal in a businesslike way, correcting in turn
Bottom, who says 'odious' instead of 'odours', and Flute: ' "Ninus'
tomb", man! – Why, you must not speak that yet. That you answer to
Pyramus. You speak all your part at once, cues and all' (Act III, Scene
1). Earlier he controls Bottom, whose determination to play every part
could otherwise wreck the entire project. Quince cleverly uses flattery
to content Bottom with the role of Pyramus: 'a sweet-faced man; a
proper man as one shall see in a summer's day' (Act I, Scene 2).

Quince also shares with the others a boundless admiration for
Bottom which casts doubt on his powers of judgement: 'You have not a
man in all Athens able to discharge Pyramus but he' (Act IV, Scene 2),
and he is quickly scared as when Bottom is 'translated' (Act III, Scene
1) by the ass' head put over his own head by Puck.

Quince's two main characteristics are simpleness and duty. In
addition to these, and within the limits of his simplicity, he also is
accommodating, shrewd and thoughtful, and manages difficult situations quite well.

35. Comment on Shakespeare's use of rhyme in *A Midsummer Night's Dream*. (A)

Generally, Shakespeare's use of rhyme was at its height in his early plays and decreased in the later work. As *A Midsummer Night's Dream* was probably written only one third of the way through his career as a dramatist, one expects to find in it considerable use of rhyme. Moreover, the nature of the subject-matter, involving the supernatural, might be expected to call for special effects that rhyme could help to achieve.

Puck, for example, always speaks in rhyme, and this is appropriate for a mischievous, spell-casting sprite. Similarly, when Oberon performs acts of magic, he speaks in rhymed verse:

> Flower of this purple dye,
> Hit with Cupid's archery,
> Sink in apple of his eye.
>
> (Act III, Scene 2)

The Fairies' songs, as befits songs, are also in rhyme. However, it is curious to note that Oberon and Titania do not always speak in rhyme. Their quarrel, in Act II, Scene 1, is entirely in blank verse, probably because Shakespeare considered rhyme inappropriate to the sentiments expressed and wanted to demonstrate how like a human married couple the Fairy King and Queen could be when angry.

Rhyme is used inconsistently in the affairs of the young lovers. One can draw a tentative conclusion about this. Possibly, Shakespeare uses rhyme to induce a dream-like effect concerning the temporary misfortunes of the lovers. In the opening scene, there is no rhyme while Egeus presents his case but the final part of the scene, involving the conspiracy of the lovers, is rhymed. Later, in the wood, Lysander and Hermia, before they sleep, and Helena and Demetrius, the pursuer and the pursued, all speak rhymed verse. Even when Hermia accuses Demetrius of murdering Lysander, Shakespeare still regards rhyme as appropriate:

> Hast thou slain him then?
> Henceforth be never numbered among men.
> O, once tell true – tell true, even for my sake.
> Durst thou have looked upon him being awake? . . . .

But when all four lovers join in the quarrel, some moments later, the use of rhyme is dropped. However, later still, as each falls asleep, the dream-like atmosphere is restored by the use of rhyme again.

The craftsmen speak in prose, as one would expect in Shakespeare, and when one of them, Bottom, becomes involved in the fairy world, the results are interesting: Titania speaks in rhymed verse and

Bottom replies in prose:

TITANIA

And thy fair virtue's force perforce doth move me,
On the first view, to say, to swear, I love thee.

BOTTOM

Methinks, mistress, you should have little reason for that.

(Act III, Scene 1)

The craftsmen's play 'Pyramus and Thisbe' is rhymed. However, this is no surprise as Shakespeare is parodying a poor type of dramatisation.

Shakespeare does not always require rhyme for specially beautiful or descriptive passages, even when they are spoken by the Fairies. Oberon's speech about Cupid's fiery shaft (Act II, Scene 1) illustrates this point.

Generally rhyme serves to create a supernatural or dream-like quality, or to differentiate the real world from the world of fantasy. This contrast is well demonstrated at the end of the play where the mortals, speaking prose depart, leaving the Fairies to speak their benedictions in rhymed verse.

36. At what times do you feel pity for (a) Hermia and (b) Helena? Explain how this pity is evoked. (A)

(a) Hermia's plight evokes our pity early in the first scene. She loves Lysander but her father has decided that she should marry Demetrius. Her father seems unnecessarily cruel about it and is obviously mistaken about Lysander's emotions when he accuses him of 'feigning' love. He is in favour of Demetrius even though Lysander's estimate of his rival as a: 'spotted and inconstant man', (Act I, Scene 1) seems reasonably accurate since he recently made love to Helena (who still dotes on him) before switching his attention to Hermia. Moreover, Athenian law is harsh. Hermia has only three choices. She must either obey her father, be executed, or become a nun:

Chanting faint hymns to the cold fruitless moon.

(Act I, Scene 1)

We pity a young girl faced with such a choice, and we admire her courage in refusing to accept the 'unwished' marriage with Demetrius. We pity her, when she is left alone with Lysander, because she is nearly in tears and because she still remains brave:

Then let us teach our trial patience

(Act I, Scene 1)

When Lysander and Hermia have taken some positive action to escape from Athenian law, we are again made to feel pity for Hermia, for they are lost and Hermia faints: 'with wandering in the wood', (Act II, Scene 2). Yet, when she awakes, we have even greater cause to pity her, for she has been deserted by Lysander, and is alone, in the darkness of the wood, troubled by a nightmare in which it seems that a serpent eats her heart away while Lysander sits smiling. Inevitably, when she finds Demetrius, she concludes that he has murdered her lover, and we can admire her resolve when she says:

> If thou hast slain Lysander in his sleep,
> Being o'er shoes in blood, plunge in the deep,
> And kill me too.

> (Act III, Scene 2)

Possibly she loses a little of our sympathy when she becomes hot-tempered with the innocent Demetrius, but her plight is no less pitiable because of that.

Later, finding the two men with Helena, she misunderstands the situation and her kindness to Helena invokes our admiration for her character:

> Sweet, do not scorn her so.

> (Act III, Scene 2)

However, when she perceives the truth of the situation, her attack against Helena is so bitter that, although we feel pity for her, we are also amused by her behaviour.

(b) Helena, too, wins our pity very early in the play. We learn from Lysander that Demetrius:

> Made love to Nedar's daughter, Helena

> (Act I, Scene 1)

and then deserted her, leaving her devoutly doting upon him. Helena's first appearance confirms the truth of this, as she yearns for the power which Hermia has to attract Demetrius, and shows us how cruelly Demetrius has treated her:

> The more I love, the more he hateth me.

> (Act I, Scene 1)

In Act II, Scene 1, we see Helena and Demetrius together in the wood. Helena is in a pathetic situation because she has informed him of Hermia and Lysander's elopement in the hope of gaining his thanks but he continues to repulse her. She informs him:

> I'll follow thee, and make a heaven of hell
> To die upon the hand I love so well.

> (Act II, Scene 1)

89

In the following scene, Demetrius finally escapes from his exhausted pursuer, making her plight all the more pitiable, since she is left alone in the now dark wood. When Lysander awakes, his unexpected declaration of love is no consolation to her, since she believes it to be:

> 'keen mockery'.

> (Act II, Scene 2)

Eventually by Act III, Scene 2, her love for Demetrius is returned through the wiles of the fairies, so in one sense her plight is no longer pitiable. Yet both pity and laughter are evoked by her behaviour, for she believes the men are both mocking her:

> If you were men, as men you are in show –
> You would not use a gentle lady so.

> (Act III, Scene 2)

Similarly, at first, her resentment at Hermia's apparent complicity with the men is touching:

> So we grew together
> Like to a double cherry, seeming parted,
> But yet an union in partition.

> (Act III, Scene 2)

Later in the same scene, her behaviour excites our pity for the last time, as she falls asleep, still believing that the others all 'detest' her, and ignorant of what her fortunes will be when she awakes.

37. 'Theseus appears in only three scenes and yet his role is very important.' Discuss. (A)

It is true that Theseus appears in only three scenes, but his role is very important in *A Midsummer Night's Dream*.

The actual scenes in which he appears are only: Act I, Scene 1, Act IV, Scene 1 and Act V, Scene 1. In the first, he speaks of his forthcoming marriage and hears the complaint of Egeus against Lysander and Hermia. In Act IV, Scene 1, he makes abortive plans for a hunt, wakens the four lovers and gives his judgement in the case concerning Hermia. In the final scene, he presides over the events and entertainment that follow the triple wedding, and is the last of the mortals to speak.

His role is important for several reasons. The story of his own love enriches the intricate pattern of love stories interwoven in the play. His love is the first to be mentioned in the play, as he eagerly looks forward to his marriage with Hippolyta. Unlike Lysander, Demetrius or even Pyramus, he won his bride as the result of defeating her in war:

> Hippolyta, I wooed thee with my sword,
> And won thy love doing thee injuries;
> But I will wed thee in another key:
> With pomp, with triumph, and with revelling.

(Act I, Scene 1)

Apart from its intrinsic interest, the role of Theseus is important to the structure of *A Midsummer Night's Dream* for it is largely due to Theseus that the various stories are so well interwoven. The young lovers, for example, owe their eventual happiness to him. He is, in Act I, Scene 1, as kind to them as the law of Athens allows, for he acknowledges Demetrius' unfaithfulness and gives Hermia three choices and reasonable time to think the matter over. In Act IV, Scene 1, he quickly recognises how well events have turned out and peremptorily declares:

> Egeus, I will overbear your will;
> For in the temple by and by, with us
> These couples shall eternally be knit.

Thus, through his intervention, the story is brought to a happy conclusion.

Similarly, it is due to his kindness and decisiveness that the Athenian craftsmen enjoy their moment of triumph. This time he overrules Philostrate. The Master of the Revels considers 'Pyramus and Thisbe' to be unworthy of the Duke's attention, but Theseus says:

> never any thing can be amiss,
> When simpleness and duty tender it.

(Act V, Scene 1)

As a result the painstaking rehearsals prove not to have been in vain, and the audience is treated to one of the funniest scenes in the whole play.

Even the story of Titania and Oberon is related to Theseus. The Fairy King and Queen are aware of his forthcoming marriage and plan to be present to give their blessing. Moreover, it happens that Titania and Oberon accuse each other of loving Theseus and Hippolyta respectively, and this is one of the causes of their quarrel.

Clearly, the role of Theseus is important for its intrinsic interest and for its function in co-ordinating the various plots and sub-plots within the play. Appropriately, of the mortals in the play, he is both first and last to speak.

38. 'In *A Midsummer Night's Dream*, several characters sleep on the stage and their sleep serves to actuate the plot.' Discuss and illustrate this statement. (A)

In Act I, no character sleeps on the stage and the plot is actuated mainly by Egeus's anger, Hermia's intention to escape, and Helena's decision to tell Demetrius of Hermia and Lysander's proposed elopement.

However, in Acts II, III and IV, there are ten occasions when a character sleeps on the stage. These serve not only to actuate the plot but also to give some of the dream-like quality to the events of these acts.

First, in Act II, Scene 2, Titania sleeps. The importance of this is that it gives Oberon the oportunity to place the love-juice on her eyes, and so torment her for refusing to surrender the changeling boy. When she wakes, she sees and loves Bottom, ass head and all.

Next Lysander and Hermia, lost and exhausted, lie down and sleep. This is very important to one of the main stories in the play, since Puck anoints Lysander's eyes with the love potion, mistaking him for Demetrius and confusion follows when Lysander awakes and the first person he sees is Helena:

> And run through fire I will for they sweet sake.

> (Act II, Scene 2)

Hermia wakes a few moments later, having had a bad dream and having lost Lysander, during only a short sleep.

In Act III, Scene 2, Demetrius, exhausted, having had no success in his pursuit of Hermia says:

> There is no following her in this fierce vein.

and he lies down. His sleep actuates the plot in a very important way, since it gives Oberon and Puck the opportunity to 'rectify' their mistake and make him love Helena. As a result two men declare their love for Helena and she at first believes neither of them. The sleep of Lysander and Demetrius, therefore, is the mainspring of a particularly lively scene.

At the end of Act III, Scene 2, all four of the lovers are made to sleep again and the result is that fantasy and reality are confused in their minds. Moreover, while they sleep, the spell is removed from Lysander, thus ensuring a happy ending to the story of the Athenian lovers. Demetrius is so surprised at how well things have turned out that he says:

> It seems to me
> That yet we sleep, we dream.

> (Act IV, Scene 1)

Earlier, in Act IV, Scene 1, another sub-plot is brought to a satisfactory conclusion as the result of the sleep of Titania and Bottom. Before Titania sleeps, she says of Bottom:

O, how I love thee! How I dote on thee!

When the spell has been removed by the rather remorseful and now satisfied Oberon, she wakes and says:

O, how mine eyes do loathe his visage now!

(Act IV, Scene 1)

As for Bottom, when he wakes from his 'dream', his ass' head has been removed and there is no further impediment to his being reunited with his anxious friends.

In all, seven characters sleep on the stage, three of them on two occasions. Their sleep, and in particular what Oberon and Puck do to them while they sleep, are very important in actuating the plots of most of the stories interwoven in *A Midsummer Night's Dream*.

CONTEXT QUESTIONS (O AND A)

39. Read the following passage and answer the questions below it.

EGEUS:
This man hath bewitched the bosom of my child.   1.
Thou, thou, Lysander, thou hast given her rhymes,
And interchanged love tokens with my child.
Thou hast by moonlight at her window sung
With feigning voice, verses of feigning love,   5.
And stolen the impression of her fantasy.
With bracelets of thy hair, rings, gauds, conceits,
Knacks, trifles, nosegays, sweetmeats – messengers
Of strong prevailment in unhardened youth.   9.

(Act I, Scene 1)

(a) When are these lines spoken?
(b) Give modern equivalents for:
   (i) 'stolen the impression of her fantasy' (line 6); (ii) 'gauds,
   conceits' (line 7).
(c) After speaking these lines, what 'ancient privilege' does Egeus
   request?
(d) What exactly is Egeus objecting to when he uses the expression
   'unhardened youth'?
(e) Summarise, *in not more than fifty words* how Theseus deals with
   the complaint of Egeus here and elsewhere in the play.

39. (a) The lines are spoken early in Act I, Scene 1, at the palace of
       Theseus in Athens.
   (b) (i) cunningly impressed your image upon her imagination;
       (ii) playthings, fanciful trinkets.
   (c) Egeus requests the ancient privilege of Athens, namely to be
       permitted to dispose of his own daughter as he wishes, either
       to Demetrius or to her death.
   (d) Egeus is objecting to the fact that, in his opinion, Hermia is
       too inexperienced ('unhardened') and too young to see that
       Lysander's love-tokens are insincere and deceptive.
   (e) Here, Theseus, has unsuccessfully urged Hermia to obey her
       father, and gives her until his own wedding-day to choose
       between death, marriage to Demetrius or becoming a nun. At
       the end of the play, because Demetrius now loves Helena,
       Theseus overrides Egeus and permits Hermia to marry
       Lysander.

40. Read the following passage and answer the questions below it.

> There sleeps Titania some time of the night,　　　1.
> Lulled in these flowers with dances and delight.
> And there the snake throws her enamelled skin,
> Weed wide enough to wrap a fairy in.
> And with the juice of this I'll streak her eyes,　　　5.
> And make her full of hateful fantasies.
> Take thou some of it, and seek through this grove.
> A sweet Athenian lady is in love
> With a disdainful youth – anoint his eyes;
> But do it when the next thing he espies
> May be this lady.　　　11.

(Act II, Scene 1)

(a) Who is the speaker?
(b) What is the occasion?
(c) Give modern equivalents for:
　　(i) 'throws' (line 3); (ii) 'weed' (line 4).
(d) Where was the 'juice' (line 5) obtained? What gave it its magical powers?
(e) How is the listener to recognise the 'disdainful youth?'
(f) Say very briefly what is done in the next scene by the speaker of the above lines.

40. (a) Oberon is speaking.
　　(b) Puck, has returned to Oberon after fetching the flower 'love-in-idleness' as instructed.
　　(c) (i) casts off (ii) garment.
　　(d) The magic juice was obtained from 'love-in-idleness'. It acquired its magical powers when it was struck, accidentally, by one of Cupid's arrows.
　　(e) Puck is to recognise Lysander by his Athenian garments.
　　(f) Oberon, weaving a spell, squeezes the juice on the eyelids of the sleeping Titania.

41. Read the following passage and answer the questions below it.

> Therefore the winds, piping to us in vain,　　　1.
> As in revenge have sucked up from the sea
> Contagious fogs which, falling in the land,
> Hath every pelting river made so proud
> That they have overborne their continents.　　　5.
> The ox hath therefore stretched his yoke in vain,
> The ploughman lost his sweat, and the green corn
> Hath rotted ere his youth attained a beard.

> The fold stands empty in the drownèd field,
> And crows are fatted with the murrion flock.   10.
> The nine men's morris is filled up with mud,
> And the quaint mazes in the wanton green
> For lack of tread are undistinguishable.   13.
>
> (Act II, Scene 1)

(a) (i) Who is the speaker?
    (ii) To whom is the speech addressed?
    (iii) At what point in the play does this speech occur?

(b) Explain the cause of the disturbances mentioned in this speech.

(c) Give modern equivalents for;
    (i) 'contagious' (line 3); (ii)'pelting' (line 4); (iii) 'overborne their continents' (line 5).

(d) What is meant by 'murrion flock' (line 10)?

(e) Say very briefly what the nine men's morris was.

(f) Mention two other unnatural events all of which we are told later in this speech.

41. (a) (i) Titania
    (ii) Oberon
    (iii) In Act II, Scene 1, the King and Queen of the Fairies have just come face to face for the first time in the play.

(b) The disturbances have been caused by the quarrel between Oberon and Titania. Titania has a 'changeling boy', the son of a 'votaress' of her order, who died at the child's birth. Oberon wants the boy to enter his own service but Titania refuses to surrender him. The quarrel also includes mutual accusations of infidelity: each accuses the other of loving mortals.

(c) (i) poisonous; (ii) paltry; (iii) burst their banks.

(d) The meaning is diseased animals.
    Murrion (now) is a disease of sheep and cattle.

(e) The nine men's morris was a game, not unlike draughts, played on squares which would be cut on the village green.

(f) Two other unnatural events are:
    (i) the formation of frost on the buds:
>   hoary-headed frosts
> Fall in the fresh lap of the crimson rose.

    (ii) the abundance of rheumatic diseases, caused by the angry moon, which makes the floods wash 'all the air'.

42. Read the following passage and answer the questions below it.

PUCK

When they him spy –	1.
As wild geese that the creeping fowler eye,	
Or russet-pated choughs, many in sort,	
Rising and cawing at the gun's report,	
Sever themselves and madly sweep the sky –	5.
So at his sight away his fellows fly,	
And at our stamp here o'er and o'er one falls.	
He 'Murder!' cries, and help from Athens calls.	
Their sense thus weak, lost with their fears thus strong,	
Made senseless things begin to do them wrong.	10.

(Act III, Scene 2)

(a) On what occasion are these words spoken? To whom is Puck speaking?

(b) In about thirty words, say who 'they' (line 1) are, and what incident Puck is describing.

(c) Explain the meaning of (i) 'russet-pated choughs' and: (ii) 'Made senseless things begin to do them wrong.'

(d) What figure of speech do you observe beginning at:'As wild geese. . . .'? How appropriate is it?

(e) In what connection is Titania mentioned, later in this speech?

42. (a) The occasion is when Oberon asks Puck for a report on whom Titania has fallen in love with as a result of the love potion. Puck is speaking to Oberon.

(b) 'They', are the craftsmen from Athens. Puck is describing the end of their rehearsal in the wood, when they scattered in terror after seeing the ass' head on Bottom.

(c) (i) grey-headed jackdaws (russet could mean grey as well as red)

(ii) caused inanimate objects [such as thorns] to harm them.

(d) The figure of speech is a simile. It is very appropriate because Bottom's friends scattered in terror, just like wild geese sensing imminent danger, or jackdaws frightened by a gunshot.

(e) Titania is mentioned later as having been awakened when Bottom was left alone near by, so she: 'straightway loved an ass.'

43. Read the following passage and answer the questions below it.

X

Out, dog! Out, cur! Thou drivest me past the bounds	1.
Of maiden's patience. Hast thou slain him then?	
Henceforth be never numbered among men.	

O, once tell true – tell true, even for my sake.
Durst thou have looked upon him being awake?   5.
And hast thou killed him sleeping? O brave touch!
Could not a worm, an adder do so much?
An adder did it; for with doubler tongue
Than thine, thou serpent, never adder stung.

Y

You spend your passion on a misprised mood.   10.
(Act III, Scene 2)

(a) (i) Who is speaker X?
    (ii) Who is speaker Y?
    (iii) At what point in the play are these words spoken?
(b) Give modern equivalents for:
    (i) 'touch' (line 6); (ii) 'worm' (line 7);
    (iii) 'on a misprised mood' (line 10).
(c) 'An adder did it'. Explain clearly what the speaker means by this.
(d) At this point in the play:
    (i) Whom does Lysander love?
    (ii) Whom does Demetrius love?
(e) Apart from Puck who overhears the above conversation? What is the importance of the fact that the conversation is overheard?

43. (a) (i) Hermia.
    (ii) Demetrius.
    (iii) Hermia has woken and found herself deserted by Lysander. Pursued by Demetrius she accuses him of having killed Lysander.
(b) (i) stroke, (ii) snake,
    (iii) in mistaken anger.
(c) Hermia is calling Demetrius an 'adder'. He is an 'adder' in the sense that he seems to have murdered Lysander in his sleep, just as an adder could have done. Moreover, like an adder, he is double-tongued, according to Hermia, because he seems to be simultaneously her lover and her enemy.
(d) (i) Helena.
    (ii) Hermia.
(e) Oberon overhears the conversation. This fact is important because Oberon deduces that Puck made a mistake when he applied the love juice. As a result, Oberon orders Puck to fetch Helena. Oberon anoints the eyes of Demetrius and later orders Puck to release Lysander from the spell.

44. Name the speaker and the person spoken of in each of the following.

(a) Thou art as wise as thou art beautiful.
(b) All fancy-sick she is and pale of cheer....
(c) Lo, she is one of this confederacy.
(d) Thou runaway, thou coward – art thou fled?
(e) Fie, fie, you counterfeit, you puppet, you!
(f) O, how I love thee! How I dote on thee!
(g) She was a vixen when she went to school.
(h) This fellow doth not stand upon points.
(i) Weeds of Athens he doth wear.
(j) O me, you juggler, you canker-blossom.

44. (a) Titania is speaking of Bottom (Act III, Scene 1)
(b) Oberon is speaking of Helena (Act III, Scene 2)
(c) Helena is speaking of Hermia (Act III, Scene 2)
(d) Demetrius is speaking of Lysander (Act III, Scene 2)
(e) Helena is speaking of Hermia (Act III, Scene 2)
(f) Titania is speaking of Bottom (Act IV, Scene 1)
(g) Helena is speaking of Hermia (Act III, Scene 2)
(h) Theseus is speaking of Quince (Act V, Scene 1)
(i) Puck is speaking of Lysander (Act II, Scene 2)
(j) Hermia is speaking of Helena (Act III, Scene 2)

45. State briefly:
   (a) Who is speaking,
   (b) What is the occasion,
   for each of the following quotations

(i) Love looks not with the eyes, but with the mind,
And therefore is winged Cupid painted blind.
Nor hath love's mind of any judgement taste;
Wings and no eyes figure unheedy haste.
(ii) To you your father should be as a god;
One that composed your beauties – yea, and one
To whom you are but as a form in wax
By him imprinted, and within his power
To leave the figure or disfigure it.
(iii) No, no – I am as ugly as a bear;
For beasts that meet me run away for fear.
(iv) I grant you, friends, if you should fright the ladies out of their wits,
they would have no more discretion but to hang us....
(v) I pray thee, gentle mortal, sing again!
Mine ear is much enamoured of thy note.

(i) (a) Helena.

    (b) She is making the last speech in Act I, Scene 1. She laments Demetrius' indifference to her and plans to tell him Hermia's secret.

(ii) (a) Theseus.

    (b) In Act I, Scene 1, Theseus is urging Hermia to submit to her father's will and marry Demetrius.

(iii) (a) Helena.

    (b) Demetrius has just escaped from Helena in the wood (Act II, Scene 2). Helena envies Hermia's beauty.

(iv) (a) Bottom.

    (b) In Act I, Scene 2, when Bottom offers himself for almost every part in the play. He says that if he plays the part of the Lion he will roar in such a way as not to frighten the ladies.

(v) (a) Titania.

    (b) In Act III, Scene 1, Titania, whose eyes have been anointed with the love juice, has just been awakened by Bottom who is singing. She falls in love with him at once.

46. Read the following passage and answer the questions below it.

> My hounds are bred out of the Spartan kind,   1.
> So flewed, so sanded; and their heads are hung
> With ears that sweep away the morning dew;
> Crook-kneed, and dewlapped like Thessalian bulls;
> Slow in pursuit, but matched in mouth like bells,   5.
> Each under each. A cry more tuneable
> Was never hallooed to nor cheered with horn
> In Crete, in Sparta, nor in Thessaly.
> Judge, when you hear. But soft, what nymphs are these?   9.
>
>   (Act IV, Scene 1)

(a) Who is the speaker and who are the 'nymphs' referred to in line 9?

(b) What explanation does the speaker, in his next speech, suggest for the presence of the 'nymphs' there?

(c) Give modern equivalents for: (i) 'flew'd' (line 2) and (ii) 'matched in mouth like bells,
Each under each.' (lines 5 and 6).

(d) Where was Sparta?

(e) What has the previous speaker said about 'hounds'?

(f) In not more than thirty words, summarise what the speaker does in the rest of this scene.

46. (a) The speaker is Theseus (in Act IV, Scene 1). The 'nymphs' are Hermia and Helena, who are asleep on the ground, near Lysander and Demetrius.

(b) Theseus' explanation for their presence is that they must have risen early:

> to observe
> The rite of May.

He also says that, as they must have known his intentions concerning a hunt, they wished to be present to grace the occasion.

(c) (i) With thick, overhanging upper lips. (ii) With their cries each fitting well with those of the other hounds, and yet being on a different pitch (like a chime of bells).

(d) Sparta, was in the southern part of Greece.

(e) The previous speaker, Hippolyta, has said that she once watched Hercules and Cadmus bring the bear to bay with hounds in Crete. To her the cries of the hounds were full of delight:

> So musical a discord, such sweet thunder.

(f) Theseus wakes the lovers and, hearing that Demetrius now loves Helena, he overrules Egeus, cancels his hunting, and sets off to arrange the triple wedding.

47. Read the following passage and answer the questions below it.

> Ay, do! Persever, counterfeit sad looks,   1.
> Make mouths upon me when I turn my back,
> Wink each at other, hold the sweet jest up.
> This sport well carried, shall be chroniclèd.
> If you have any pity, grace, or manners,   5.
> You would not make me such an argument.
> But fare ye well. 'Tis partly my own fault,
> Which death or absence soon shall remedy.   8.
>
> (Act III, Scene 2)

(a) Who is the speaker?

(b) Name all the other characters who are on the stage when these words are spoken.

(c) In what way is the speaker mistaken?

(d) Give modern equivalents for: (i) 'make mouths' (line 2); (ii) 'argument' (line 6).

(e) Outline very briefly what happens after this speech, up to the end of the scene.

47. (a) Helena.

(b) Hermia, Lysander, Demetrius, Oberon and Puck.

(c) Helena believes that Lysander and Demetrius do not really love her, and are only pretending to do so, as a practical joke. She also believes that Hermia is a party to the joke.

(d) (i) make mocking faces; (ii) Subject for mockery.

(e) The men continue to declare their love. Hermia becomes convinced that Lysander really does love Helena, so she attacks Helena. The women almost come to blows and the men decide to fight a duel for the love of Helena. Finally, Oberon and Puck prevent actual bloodshed, cause all four lovers to go to sleep, and remove the effect of the love juice from Lysander.

48. Give, in one sentence each, the contexts of the following quotations.

(a)   Come, wait upon him. Lead him to my bower.
The moon methinks looks with a watery eye;
And when she weeps every little flower,
Lamenting some enforcèd chastity.

(b)   Truly, a peck of provender. I could munch your good dry oats.

(c)   Now thou and I are new in amity,
And will tomorrow midnight solemnly
Dance in Duke Theseus' house triumphantly,
And bless it to all fair prosperity.

(d)   Lovers and madmen have such seething brains,
Such shaping fantasies, that apprehend
More than cool reason ever comprehends.

(e)   How happy some o'er other some can be!
Through Athens I am thought as fair as she.

48. (a) At the end of Act III, Scene 1, Titania is ordering her fairies to escort Bottom to her bower.
  (b) Bottom, offered food by Titania, in Act IV, Scene 1, is stating what he desires.
  (c) In Act IV, Scene 1, Oberon is now reconciled with Titania, whom he has released from a charm, and plans to attend and bless the wedding of Theseus.
  (d) At the beginning of Act V, Scene 1, Theseus is sceptical about the story the lovers have told and is telling Hippolyta how lovers, like madmen and poets, let their imaginations run away with them.
  (e) Helena, alone at the end of Act I, Scene 1, envies Hermia, who is not generally thought more beautiful than herself, but who is loved by Demetrius.

REVISION QUESTIONS ON
A MIDSUMMER NIGHT'S DREAM

R.S.A., C.S.E., O LEVEL AND 16+

1. How does Shakespeare convey an impression of the lightness and grace of the fairy world?

2. Give a full account of Bottom's 'translation' and its consequences.

3. What do we learn from *A Midsummer Night's Dream* about Shakespeare's knowledge and appreciation of the English countryside?

4. Which scene do you like best? Give reasons for your choice.

5. 'Bottom is ever resourceful.' Give examples of his resourcefulness.

6. Write a character study of Helena.

7. What do you admire about (a) Theseus, and (b) Oberon?

8. Whom do you regard as more important, Oberon or Theseus? Give reasons for your choice.

9. Quote a passage of striking beauty and show why you admire it.

10. Could *A Midsummer Night's Dream* be more successful as a film than as a theatre play? Give reasons for your opinions.

11. If you had to produce *A Midsummer Night's Dream* and were forced to leave parts out, which would you choose? Give reasons for your answer.

12. How far do you find the following qualities in Lysander: a sense of humour; bravery; coolness of temper?

13. Show how the story of the Athenian craftsmen is interwoven with the other stories in *A Midsummer Night's Dream*.

14. Which scene in the play does most to develop the plot? Which does least? Give reasons for your choice.

15. What is the dramatic importance of (a) Egeus, and (b) Philostrate?

16. 'She was a vixen when she went to school.' If Helena's words about Hermia are correct, how much has Hermia changed since her schooldays?

17. What does Theseus say about children's duties towards their fathers?

18. How far do you consider Puck to be (a) helpful, and (b) amiable?

19. Explain why Lysander and Helena both hate Hermia, in Act III, Scene 2.

20. Summarise the various attitudes to love and marriage expressed in the play.

21. From two different scenes describe two incidents which you find particularly amusing. Explain why they are so funny.

22. How many of the following do you consider make mistakes during the play: Puck; Lysander; Egeus; Theseus? In what ways are their mistakes made?

23. What is amusing in the behaviour of Oberon and Titania?

24. Summarise the occasions on which spells are cast or removed and indicate the various consequences.

A LEVEL

25. With particular references, examine the love-speeches of Demetrius and Lysander and comment on the use of figurative language.

26. Consider the importance and use of music in *A Midsummer Night's Dream.*

27. 'A miscellany of midsummer madness.' Consider this view of the sources of *A Midsummer Night's Dream.*

28. 'A truly imaginative, unreal world.' Consider this view of Shakespeare's fairy world.

29. 'The supernatural is an essential part of *A Midsummer Night's Dream.*' Discuss.

30. 'Many of the incidents are preposterous without any hope of verisimilitude.' Discuss this criticism of *A Midsummer Night's Dream.*

31 'Ethereal and theatrical.' Consider this view of *A Midsummer Night's Dream.*

32. 'The best portrait of the Elizabethan tradesman.' Discuss this view of Bottom.

33. 'The King of Shadows.' Consider Oberon's character and personality in the light of this statement.

34. 'Shakespeare has succeeded in making his fairies satisfyingly whole.' Discuss with close reference to *A Midsummer Night's Dream*.

35. 'The mischievous goblin.' Consider this view of Puck.

36. 'Literary contrivance, anachronism and classical allusion ruin *A Midsummer Night's Dream*. Examine this stricture by careful reference to the play.

37. 'More a masque than a play.' Examine the truth of this statement on *A Midsummer Night's Dream.*

38. 'The whole thing swarms with enchantment' (Hudson). Discuss this view of *A Midsummer Night's Dream.*

39. '*A Midsummer Night's Dream* is in the true sonnet tradition of Shakespearean England'. Explain this statement.

40. 'A play full of lyrical language and rustic prose'. By close reference to the play, examine this statement.

41. Consider the aptness of the imagery in *A Midsummer Night's Dream*.

42. Examine the use of either (a) rhymed or (b) blank verse in *A Midsummer Night's Dream*.

43. Give an account of the 'rude mechanicals' in *A Midsummer Night's Dream*.

44. Explain how Shakespeare contrasts the fairy world with the world of mortals in the play.

45. 'One of the greatest of all Shakespeare's characters'. Consider this view of Theseus.

46. 'The play can be divided into three character groups which are harmoniously blended'. Discuss this statement on *A Midsummer Night's Dream*.

47. 'A play about incident, not character'. Consider this view of *A Midsummer Night's Dream*.

48. 'A comedy dependent on poetic contrivance and beautiful settings'. Discuss.

49. Do you consider the songs as an important part of the play? Give reasons for your opinions.

50. Explain the importance of the story of Pyramus and Thisbe in *A Midsummer Night's Dream*.

51. 'Despite our disbelief we almost believe in Shakespeare's fairies.' Show how far you agree with this statement by close reference to *A Midsummer Night's Dream*.

THE LITERATURE EXAMINATION

If you have properly prepared you need not fear the actual examination. The evening before it is to take place read over all the notes you have made during the year, paying special attention to your summaries. You will find, because you have made these summaries, that you will be able to read through all your set books (in outline). Do not stay up too late, and get enough sleep.

On the day of the examination get to the examination room on time. Remember the following points.

1. Read through the paper carefully. Make sure you read every question. Mark those you think you can do.

2. Make sure you read the rubrics (the instructions). In most literature papers there is a compulsory question. This is usually of the context type. It is wisest to do this first, for if you leave it until the end you might find you do not have time to complete it.

3. You should plan your time carefully. Normally, the O Level paper lasts for 2½ hours and you are to answer five questions. Do not take longer than 25 minutes over each question, and leave the last 25 minutes to read over your work.

4. After the context or compulsory question has been answered (if any), answer what you consider to be the easiest question. You should then proceed to the more difficult ones.

5. Write in clear, straightforward English. Do not use abbreviations except in actual words spoken, and avoid slang, clichés and colloquial writing.

6. Make sure that you understand what the examiner wants before you answer. If you are not sure, try another question. One of the main causes of failure at examinations is irrelevancy – students do NOT answer the question set.

7. Quotations are essential in English Literature. However, they must be accurate and to the point. If your quotations do not illustrate the point you are trying to make, then they are useless. If you are given a poem to criticise and it is written out for you on the question paper, do not waste the examiner's time by quoting from it. A good idea is to number the lines if you want to refer to it. When personal reactions are called for, there is no need to quote.

8. There is no need to write at length. Two to two and a half sides are normally adequate for an essay-type question. When answering context questions keep your answers short and to the point. Re-read what has been said about these earlier in this book.

9. There is no need to write out the questions. However, make sure you number your answers correctly.

10. Write legibly and avoid crossing out. If you must cross out work because you feel that you can do better on another question, one straight line through the work you do not want marked is enough.

11. There is no need to write a lengthy introductory paragraph.

12. If a question is divided into two or more parts or sections, you should pay equal attention to each. Often candidates write at length on one part or section and dismiss the other/s in a few lines.

13. Do not write descriptions unless requested. Do not recount the story unless asked. Some candidates give 'an account of', 'describe' or 'outline' when a critical approach is required.

14. The names of the main characters in your set books should be spelt correctly. Similarly, the names of the authors, titles of essays and poems, should be remembered if you are to use them in the examination. Words like 'playwright' and 'Shakespeare' are often misspelt.

15. If you have consulted any authorities on the set books and you want to refer to them, do not be afraid to do so. However, it is important to report what they have said accurately.

16. If you have your own ideas on the literature you are studying and these ideas are sensible and can be supported by quotation and reasoning, by all means express them. Remember that strange interpretations may be frowned on.

17. Do not be too critical of the writer or dramatist for being 'out of date' or having misconceptions that you know to be wrong. Avoid making hasty 20th century judgements on literature of other times.

18. If there are a number of views or interpretations on a particular scene or poem, you should be aware of these. However, you should not be afraid to give your own judgement, wherever possible giving reasons for your opinion.

19. Do not waste your time or your examiner's by making pedestrian statements, e.g., '*Hamlet* is a great tragedy' or 'Wordsworth is a famous poet'. It should not be necessary to use the same material for more than one answer.

20. Remember what is required throughout the examination is to show:

> that you know the book,
> that you understand the text,
> that you can use the knowledge correctly and apply it in answering the questions set,
> that you can select material wisely,
> that you can keep to the point,
> and that you can express your views on the book in question.

LITERARY TERMS

It is important for students to have a knowledge of the main literary terms. Dictionaries of these terms are readily available in every public or reference library. A few of the most important terms are given below.

1. **Act:** – the main division of a drama. Some writers do not use acts but a varying number of scenes instead (e.g., Galsworthy in "Escape"). The one-act play has also been developed.

2. **Allegory:** – a narrative in which the characters and incidents have a greater significance, usually moral or ideal, than appears on the surface (e.g., Bunyan's "Pilgrim's Progress").

3. **Alliteration:** – the recurrence of the same consonant sound in words close together, e.g., "The clanging bell pealed loudly". In this, the repetition of the 'l' sound.

4. **Allusion:** – reference to matters outside the work being studied.

5. **Ambiguity:** – having two meanings.

6. **Anachronism:** – a mistake in dating. For example, a playwright writing about a time B.C. refers to a watch; reference in a play of 1800 to a car.

7. **Anagram:** – a re-arrangement of a sentence or the letters of a word to form others.

8. **Anecdote:** – a short story.

9. **Anthology:** – a collection of poems.

10. **Anti-Climax** (also called bathos): – the spoiling of a climax (see no. 27 below) by the addition of a phrase or word which spoils the effect, e.g.,

    Here thou, great Anna! whom three realms obey,
    Dost sometimes counsel take — and sometimes tea.
    (Pope:- "Rape of the Lock")

11. **Antithesis:** – the placing of ideas side by side for contrast, e.g., *If they were unacquainted with the works of philosophers and poets, they were deeply read in the oracles of God.*
    (Macaulay:- "Essay on Milton")

12. **Antonyms:** – words opposite in meanings to others, e.g., good, bad.

13. (a) **Apostrophe:** – a punctuation mark indicating possession or omission, e.g., it's – it is, the woman's hat – the hat belonging to the woman.

(b) **Apostrophe:** – a turning away from the subject being considered, to address a person (or object) who (which) cannot reply, e.g.,

While thou art pouring forth thy soul abroad
In such an ecstasy!

(Keats:- "Ode to a Nightingale")

14. **Aside:** – a remark made by an actor for the audience to hear but which is meant to remain unheard by the other characters on the stage.

15. **Assonance:** – the repetition of a vowel sound in words close together, e.g., Keats' "Ode to Autumn" – "Thy hair soft-lifted by the winnowing wind". Repetition of the vowels 'i', 'o'.

16. **Atmosphere**: – the part of a written work (play, poem or prose) which gives the setting and mood of a place or scene.

17. **Ballad:** – a story expressed in simple language formerly intended to be sung.

18. **Bibliography:** – either a study of books or a list of books.

19. **Blank Verse:** – verse which does not rhyme.

20. **Bombast:** – writing in which the words used are elevated and elegant but the subject is commonplace.

21. **Burlesque:** – humour obtained from imitating a more serious work. There is usually a contrast between style and subject.

22. **Caricature:** – making fun by exaggerating a person's characteristics.

23. **Character:** – the qualities which a person has (or lacks). N.B., not merely the physical appearance of the individual concerned.

24. **Circumlocution:** – not getting to the point.

25. **Classicism:** – a love of the great writers of Greece and Rome. Also a type of writing which imitates them.
Elements of classicism – ordinary subjects; little imagination; epigrams; wit and satire; down to earth.

26. **Cliché:** – stereotyped phrases that are used too often and have therefore lost their appeal, e.g., "like two peas in a pod".

27. (a) **Climax:** – this is the decisive moment in a plot. The reader or spectator has been taken through a series of events which now reach a crisis.

    (b) **Climax:** – words, phrases or ideas put in ascending order, e.g., I came, I saw, I conquered.

28. **Coherence:** – ability to write poetry or prose consistently in a logical, connected sequence.

29. **Colloquialism:** – using words in or from ordinary speech, e.g., don't, 'bus, 'cab and exam'.

30. **Comedy:** – drama which ends happily. Usually a comedy contains humour.

31. **Consonance:** – sound harmony or use of vowel sounds at the end of lines followed consistently by the same consonants.

32. **Counterplot:** – a type of sub-plot similar to, or in contrast with, the main plot. This is usually introduced to add point to the main plot.

33. **Coup de théâtre:** – an unexpected or surprising development in a play.

34. **Couplet:** – two-rhymed lines of verse.

35. **Dénouement:** – how a playwright unravels the complications of the plot of a play.

36. **Deus ex Machina:** – an expected event which solves a difficult problem.

37. **Dialogue:** – conversation between two people.

38. **Didacticism:** – an attempt made in writing to instruct, especially in matters of taste, morals and ideals.

39. **Doggerel:** – simple verse which is often cynical and intends to be humorous.

40. **Double-negative:** – using two negatives, e.g., "I do not know nothing". (This is a device often found in Shakespearean plays.)

41. **Dramatic irony:** – in which the words spoken on the stage have more significance for the audience than the characters involved in the play.

42. **Dramatic monologue:** – either a poem in which a speaker recounts his experiences or thoughts (e.g., Tennyson's "Locksley Hall") or a dramatic speech monopolised by one person. (If

the latter the actor is conscious that there is an audience. Contrast soliloquy no. 95 below.)

43. **Elegy:** – a short verse concerned with death or love.

44. **Epic:** – a long poem telling a story and written in a high-flown style, e.g., Milton's "Paradise Lost".

45. **Epigram:** – a short, pointed saying.

46. **Episode:** – a device used in narrative poetry in which the main story is put aside for a time to report on a particular person or event.

47. **Epithalamium:** – a marriage song.

48. **Euphemism:** – a figure of speech substituting a milder expression for an unpleasant one, e.g., He died – **He passed away.**

49. **Euphuism:** – an affected and highly artificial way of writing containing too many figures of speech, and using antithesis, epigram and other devices of style. The word is taken from John Lyly's "Euphues".

50. **Exposition:** – the explaining done by an author to 'set the scene' for readers, actors or audience.

51. **Fable:** – a short story with a moral.

52. **Farce:** – humour mainly dependent upon exaggeration and meant to cause laughter.

53. **Fine-writing:** – a type of journalese which involves the use of unusual words.
(see no. 64 below.)

54. **Finished style:** – writing characterised by very great care and planning. There are few mannerisms and the writing 'flows' easily.

55. **Foreword:** – an introduction to a book explaining its objects and limits. 'Preface' is a synonym for foreword but the latter is more widely used nowadays.

56. **Genre:** – a **type** of literary work. Means 'type'.

57. **Homonyms:** – words identical in form but with different meanings, e.g. minute, minute, (one means small; the other a short period of time).
N.B., homonyms are spelt the same.

58. **Homophones:** – words that sound the same but are spelt differently and have different meanings, e.g., stationery, stationary; principal, principle.

59. **Hyperbole:** – exaggeration for emphasis, e.g., John ran as fast as greased lightning.

60. **Idyll:** – a poem giving 'a small picture' of simple country life, e.g., William Wordsworth's "The Solitary Reaper".

61. **Inversion:** – a change in the normal order of words (subject, verb, object) in a sentence, usually for sake of emphasis, e.g., "Then like a chorus, the passion deepened", (De Quincey: "Confessions of an Opium Eater").

62. **Irony:** – words are used but the idea intended to be gathered is different from the literal meaning. E.g., to say to a dull student, 'You are a clever boy!'

63. **Jargon:** – the excessive use of stereotyped words, technical terms and expressions often difficult for the layman to understand.

64. **Journalese:** – a style of writing characterised by clichés, latinized words, mixed metaphors and jargon. This 'affected' writing was typical of early journalists, hence the name.

65. **Letters:** – writing of a personal nature not intended for publication.

66. **Limerick:** – a form of nonsense verse consisting of a five-lined stanza rhyming a a b b a and with the third and fourth lines being a foot shorter than the other.

67. **Litotes:** – understatement for emphasis, e.g., He was a citizen of no mean city.

68. **Lyric:** – this is the most common of the three types of verse. The lyrical poem has musical qualities and is usually concerned with the thoughts, emotions, moods or feelings of the poet. (The other two main forms of poetry are (a) narrative – which tells a story, (b) dramatic verse – which forms a play).

69. **Malapropism:** – using the wrong word in context, e.g., 'I would not wish a daughter of mine to be a **progeny** (prodigy) of learning' (Mrs. Malaprop in Sheridan's play "The Rivals").

70. **Metaphor:** – an expressed or implied comparison, e.g.,
Expressed: (a) the camel is the ship of the desert. A camel is compared with a ship.

116

Implied: (b) the moon sails across the midnight sky. Comparison between the moon and a ship.

71. **Metonymy:** – attributes are substituted for actual names of things, e.g., **"The kettle is boiling"** (instead of the water in the kettle). "He is addicted **to the bottle**" (instead of alcoholic drinks). See Shirley's poem "Death the Leveller".

72. **Monologue:** – a speech by one person in the presence of other characters on the stage.

73. **Ode:** – this was originally any kind of poem written to be sung to music. It is now a lyric which has (a) dignity of language, (b) dignity of mood, (c) a high level of emotion, (d) seriousness. The ode has no distinctive form.

74. **Onomatopœia:** – sense suggested by the sound of the words used, e.g., chatter; rustle.

75. **Oxymoron:** – combining of contradictory words and phrases together for effect, e.g., eloquent silence, cruel kindness.

76. **Paradox:** – something which seems absurd but is in reality true, e.g., in England if you drive on the left side of the road, you are right.

77. **Parody:** – an imitation of another literary work.

78. **Pathetic fallacy:** – in which nature is made to sympathise with a person's feelings – e.g., happy – sunshine; sad – rain.

79. **Pathos:** – the emotions you feel; usually refers to feelings of pity.

80. **Periphrasis:** – using a roundabout expression instead of a straightforward one; similar to circumlocution.

81. **Personification:** – a comparison which gives inanimate objects the qualities of people, e.g., "the **arms** of a tree" instead of the branches; "The tawny-hided desert crouches watching her", (Thorpe's 'The Mirage').

82. **Picaresque:** – a type of novel which depicts the adventures of the main character of the novel who is usually something of a rogue.

83. **Poetic Justice:** – when someone who has done evil is rewarded by evil; when someone who has done good is rewarded by good.

84. **Prologue:** – a small piece of writing placed before a drama. An introduction to it.

85. **Prose:** – ordinary writing as opposed to poetry or verse.

86. **Pun:** – a play on words which is meant to be humorous. e.g., "not on thy sole, but on thy soul, harsh Jew", (Shakespeare). The first 'sole' refers to the bottom of a shoe; the second to man's after-life.

87. **Quotation:** – the use by a writer of words taken from the books of another person.

88. **Rhetorical Question:** – a question which does not require an answer, e.g., "The doves who have not laboured nor travailed in thought possess the sunlight. Is not theirs the preferable portion?" (R. Jeffries: 'The Life of the Fields').

89. **Rhyme:** – repetition of the same sound, usually at the end of lines in poetry.

90. **Rhythm:** – the 'beat' used in writing, especially in poetry.

91. **Romanticism:** – literature characterised by individualism and which is against rules and conventions in writing. Elements of romanticism include love of nature: interest in the underdog; also artificiality of diction and an attempt to obtain perfection.

92. **Satire:** – certain aspects of society or a person's character are held up to ridicule in an attempt at reform.

93. **Simile:** – a comparison usually introduced by 'like' or 'as': e.g., the warrior was **as fierce as a lion.**

94. **Slang:** – spoken words not considered fit for literary use, e.g., 'flicks' – cinema; 'bird' – girl; 'pop' – popular.

95. **Soliloquy:** – a literary device when a person is made to talk to himself so that the audience can 'read his thoughts'. Other actors are not present on the stage. The speaker is **not** conscious of an audience.

96. **Sonnet:** – a poem of 14 lines of iambic pentameters (five beats to a line). A sonnet is divided into an octave (the first eight lines) and a sestet (the last six lines). The former usually includes the main thought or description and the latter is a comment upon it. Between the octave and sestet there is a well marked pause (usually at the end of the eighth line) which is usually accompanied by a turn in the thought.

97. **Stanza:** – a verse of poetry.

98. **Style:** – the particular way in which each author writes.

99. **Sub-plot:** – a part of a story separate from the main one.

100. **Suspense:** – a device which keeps the audience in a state of expectancy.

101. **Synechdoche:** – a figure of speech in which the part is used for the whole, or the whole for the part, e.g., **England** fared badly against the **West Indian** bowling.

102. **Synonyms:** – words similar in meaning, e.g., brave, courageous.

103. **Tautology:** – repetition of an idea already expressed, e.g., final conclusion.

104. **Tragedy:** – human conflict ending in suffering.

105. **Vernacular:** – the use of ordinary, everyday language, rather than latinised language.

NOTES